OHIO TIKI

OHIO TIKI

Polynesian Idols, Coconut Trees and Tropical Cocktails

JEFF CHENAULT

Foreword by Doug Motz

THE
History
PRESS

Published by The History Press
Charleston, SC
www.historypress.com

Copyright © 2019 by Jeff Chenault

All rights reserved

First published 2019

Manufactured in the United States

ISBN 9781467142472

Library of Congress Control Number: 2019950044

This book is dedicated to Deb Chenault for believing in me and our beloved cat of fifteen years, Tiki.

CONTENTS

FOREWORD

I'll always have the good fortune to have all of my treasured Tiki memories stem from a trip to the Kahiki Supper Club in Columbus when I was seven years old. That neighborhood Polynesian wonderland transported me to realms I had never dreamed of and cast a spell that continues to enchant me and all Buckeye Tikiphiles to this day.

Since that time, over four decades have passed, and I've gotten to travel all over the state of Ohio and the country. While visiting a new city, I always do my best to seek out a Tiki bar. Trader Sam's in Los Angeles, the Tonga Room in San Francisco, Porco's in Cleveland and my own city's current offering of the delightful Grass Skirt are some of my favorites, but when I had the chance to fly to Fort Lauderdale for a business trip, I knew I had to spend an evening at the venerable Mai-Kai upon which the Kahiki was based. Even as I write this, my eyes are tearing up a bit, because when I entered that amazing Florida Tiki palace, I was immediately transported back to the Kahiki experiencing the wonder and allure that these restaurants radiate. These Polynesian palaces hold immense power; they cast a hypnotic spell over all of those who are willing to be enchanted by magic, wonder and make-believe. For those of us in Ohio, away from palm trees, hibiscus flowers and tropical trade winds, the allure of these places is even more gratifying, as they are an escape from gray winters and flat landscapes. They take us to the fantastic land of exotic cocktails, mysterious décor and magical Tiki gods!

This is how it all began for me, and I imagine my experience isn't dissimilar from those of the Buckeye readers of this book. In 1973, my mother took my Cub Scout troop on a field trip to the Kahiki to assist us in getting a badge for one thing or another. As a second grader, I had never traveled any farther than the Baskin-Robbins Ice Cream shop down the street from us, so that first trip to the magical realm of Polynesia was seared onto my memory. My first recollection is of standing in front of the largest building I had ever seen in my life at that point. The design of the five-story building was based on men's meetinghouses in New Guinea, and the details featured along the curved roof were based on the many war canoes found in the same region. The pelicans and fish that lined the apex of the roof were thought to symbolize plentiful amounts of good food. Two replica Easter Island heads stood guard at the doorway, which was also lined with Oceanic murals to ward away evil spirits. Upon entering the restaurant, the fountain "George" greeted patrons with dry ice fog flowing out of its mouth—or at least that's how I saw it. There were long, seemingly endless windows along the right-hand side of the restaurant that somehow showcased a thunderstorm in a tropical rainforest every twenty minutes. I was overwhelmed by the wonder and majesty of it all—this was Ohio after all—I had never seen anything so truly magical in my life.

When I looked left, past the singing birds, I saw rows upon rows of exotic saltwater fish swimming in tanks along the opposite wall—I was gobsmacked. I looked down the center of the restaurant and saw that it was organized by huts that reminded me of the *Gilligan's Island* reruns we sometimes watched on TV. I half-expected Gilligan or the Skipper to come around the corner during our visit, and I kept looking over my shoulder throughout the day to see where they were. As we walked through what I later found out was called the "village," we came to the giant fireplace at the other end of the restaurant that was shaped like an Easter Island head. The mouth of the head was the opening of the fireplace, and immediately next to it was a giant gong. I didn't know about the Mystery Girl and the role the gong played in summoning a lovely *wahini* server carrying sixteen ounces of flaming decadence called the "Mystery Bowl" until much later.

Patrons of the Kahiki were immersed in the world of South Seas Polynesia, and while there, they could order their choice of exotic fare and island drinks. The Kahiki offered up such drinks as the Malayan Mist, Blue Hurricane, Instant Urge, Maiden's Prayer, Misty Isle, Jungle Fever, Head Hunter, Zombie and the Smoking Eruption. Each cocktail was served in its own sculpted mug, which patrons could then purchase from the gift shop and keep as a souvenir to remind them of their visit.

Of all the memories of that glorious first visit that I have, the one I always come back to is that of the bathroom sink. As a part of our field trip, the Kahiki's staff members made a small meal for us to enjoy, but my mom insisted that we wash our hands first. Upon entering that incredible washroom, I came face to face with a giant clam-shell sink that ingrained itself into my being and summed up the entire experience. I washed my hands in the giant shell with liquid soap, and it completely captivated me. Those memories stayed with me, and after the Kahiki was demolished, my husband and I scoured flea markets, antique stores and, of course, eBay to get our hands on all things Tiki. We wanted to recreate the restaurant's sense of wonder and illusion in our own home. With the help of so many good friends, we built our own Tiki bar, Shipwreck Shirley's, in our central Ohio basement. It serves as a bastion against the everyday, and as of this writing, we invite our extended *ohana* to join us monthly for Mai Tais, exotica on the Hi-Fi and the occasional Mystery Girl or Mystery Boy to chase away the winter blues and to invite an offering of laughter, companionship and good cheer to the Tiki gods and goddesses of old.

So, a huge *MAHALO* to my good friend Jeff for sharing the stories that he has collected from every quadrant of our beloved Buckeye State and for allowing me the opportunity to again share one of my own. It is my sincere hope that his stories transport you back to a time where magic was real, exotica music filled the air and rum flowed freely from the bygone Tiki bars that once dotted the Ohio landscape.

—Doug Motz

PREFACE

I was introduced to Tiki culture through my love of exotica music, the faux jungle music that transforms everyday Tiki bars into virtual time machines. It's the key ingredient to bringing the Polynesian décor and tropical cocktails to life. It is a prefabricated world created by the purveyors of mid-century pop culture. It's not about authenticity, it's about fun and escapism. When you live in Ohio, sometimes an escape is just what you need. Who wouldn't want something that removes you from your daily routine to instantly transport you to a South Seas tropical paradise?

Ohio Tiki is an illustrated passport to the Polynesian craze of the 1950s and 1960s. It is an essential guide to the art of culinary exotica and a fascinating look into a bygone era that perpetuated the mythology of Polynesian Pop with the allure of hula girls, palm trees and Tiki gods. Hundreds of Tiki-themed restaurants, hotels, strip clubs and even bowling alleys sprung up overnight during its heyday. The key ingredient and overall appeal of these places was "atmosphere."

In the beginning, there was pre-Tiki. These places were established in the 1930s and 1940s and were tropical and Polynesian in style, but they existed before the Hawaiian craze of the 1950s and 1960s—it was a different time. People were just recovering from the Great Depression, and by 1934, with the end of Prohibition, the party was on. They didn't have exotica music, but they did have Hawaiian steel guitars that were extremely popular. Some of this interest in Polynesian culture originated from the Oahu Publishing Company, which was not located in Hawaii but Cleveland, Ohio. When

author James Michener's book *South Pacific* was published in 1947, it created a nationwide interest in Hawaiian culture. Michener's book was later adapted into a Broadway play in 1949 and then an award-winning film in 1958. Before *South Pacific*, Thor Heyerdahl's film *Kon-Tiki* won the Academy Award for Best Documentary in 1951, and it sparked the imagination of young explorers everywhere. In 1951, Les Baxter released a ten-inch record for Capitol Records called *Le Sacre du Sauvage* or "Ritual of the Savage"; its liner notes described the record's music as a "tone poem of the sound and the struggle of the jungle…the hue and mood of the interior… the tempo and texture of the bustling seaports and the Tropics!" While Les's lush version of "Quiet Village" was popular, it didn't become a huge hit until Martin Denny streamlined the Baxter originals into a jazz combo, complete with exotic percussion and soothing bird calls. The addition of frog, bird and jungle sounds sparked the nation's imagination and started a national craze. By 1959, "Quiet Village" was on the top of the musical charts, and Hawaii became our fiftieth state. The stage was being set for one of the most popular and longest enduring trends in American history.

During the early 1960s, themed restaurants were extremely popular, and the South Seas motif was the wildest theme of them all. With the success of supper clubs like the Mai Kai in Fort Lauderdale and the Kahiki in Columbus, restaurants all over United States jumped on the Polynesian bandwagon. National hotel chains all had their own Polynesian restaurants built; the Hilton chain had Trader Vic's, the Sheraton had the Kon-Tiki and the Marriott had the Kona Kai. Tiki was everywhere! Many of these places were short-lived, but others continued to ride the Polynesian wave right into the 1980s and beyond. Today, new modern Tiki bars are opening up across the country, ushering in a new resurgence of Polynesian fervor.

In this book, I have tried to document all of the known Tiki establishments that existed in the state of Ohio from 1934 to the present. This has proved to be a daunting task. Just about every small town in the state had a Hawaiian-themed restaurant or establishment. Most of these places weren't as elaborate as the Kahiki, but they were still fun places to eat, drink, socialize and, more importantly, escape. In my research, I discovered many places

Above: Sheet Music for Les Baxter's "Quiet Village," the theme song for all things exotic. *Author's collection.*

Opposite: An original *South Pacific* program from the R.K.O. Palace Theatre in Columbus, Ohio, dated March 31, 1952. *Author's collection.*

that were exotic in name only, like the Port O' Call Motor Inn in Cleveland or the Beachcomber Motor Lodge in Lorain. Both of these locations were devoid of any Polynesian atmosphere. Almost every town had a Castaways or Beachcomber bar, and some places had little to no information whatsoever of their histories except for a faded matchbook or an old newspaper advertisement. In fact, I could not include a lot of images I found due to their inferior print quality. I've included a few Chinese restaurants, because they offered something truly unique like Hawaiian décor, Tiki mugs and extraordinary cocktail menus. I even found information on places that were planned but never built.

Join me on a journey to the tropical shores of Ohio's finest Polynesian restaurants and beyond.

ACKNOWLEDGEMENTS

I am deeply indebted to Scott Schell, who joined me in my quest to find all things Tiki in Ohio. His extensive knowledge and library dedicated to Ohio and Tiki culture really helped me bring this book together. I would also like to thank author, friend and fellow Tikiphile Doug Motz for graciously writing the foreword. To Sven Kirsten and Otto von Stroheim, I would like to send thanks for their words of wisdom, inspiration and lasting friendship. Lastly, I would like to thank all of my friends in the Tiki community: Jeff "Beachbum" Berry, Mark Bloom, Bob Brooks, Natalie Rudin-Cohn, Pablus Digitalis, Don Drennan, Leslie Baxter-Eaton, Ken Holewczyski, John Holt, Lee Joseph, Jane Keller, King Kukulele, Dave Larsen, Travis Lewis, Francis Llacuna, Craig Long, Darren Patrick Long, Gerline Lude, Marty Lush, David Meyers, Carmen Owens, Mario and Armida Padilla, Todd Popp, Maggie Rickard, Jim and Elise Robinson, Dan Rockwell, Bill Sapp, Linda Sapp-Long, Joe Shuster, Eric Simon, Lena Simonian, Vern Stoltz, Tim Tetzlaff, Matt Thatcher, Humhumu Trott, Sam Walker, Elise Meyers-Walker, Christie White, Randy Wong, the Fraternal Order of Moai and, of course, Tiki Central. Thanks for sharing the fun!

1

COLUMBUS

Tiki has deep roots in Columbus. The city was home to one of the grandest Polynesian restaurants in the world, the Kahiki Supper Club. For almost forty years, the Kahiki reigned supreme in Columbus and solidified its place in Tiki history. At least two generations have fond memories of the Kahiki, one of the most beautiful restaurants in the world; famous actors, businessmen and weary travelers all visited her shores. The local theater company, the Kenley Players, had their own table (#51) in front of the giant Tiki god fireplace so actors and locals could mingle and share tropical cocktails. In 2000, when the Kahiki's voyage was nearing its end, Otto von Stroheim decided to throw the largest Tiki party ever. He called it the "Bon Voyage, Kahiki" party, and it was a party that would change the course of Tiki forever. It was the first large-scale Tiki gathering of its kind, and Sven Kirsten's *Book of Tiki*, which premiered there, ushered in a newfound appreciation for Tiki culture that still exists today. Columbus is also the birthplace of the Fraternal Order of Moai (FOM); the Kahiki chapter was founded in 2005. In the beginning, the FOM was a way for people who loved Polynesian culture to come together and share drinks and stories of our once-glorious past. Today, the FOM boasts chapters nationwide, and they donate the proceeds from various Tiki events to educational grants for Easter Island residents and local charities here in the United States.

Multiple Tiki-related events have been held in Columbus over the years. In 1992, Columbus hosted the Ameriflora '92 event that featured a pop-up Polynesian restaurant called the Hawaii Kai. In May 2010, Hills Market hosted a Hawaiian luau as a tribute to the beloved Kahiki. It was a grand

A Fraternal Order of Moai bumper sticker featuring the Kahiki Fireplace. *Courtesy of the Fraternal Order of Moai.*

event held outside, with entertainment from Curtis Silva and Francis Llacuna. In March 2015, artists Eric Immelt, Lena Simonian and Todd Hickerson organized one of the first Tiki art shows in Columbus called Modern Primitiva. It was held at the Clayspace/Gallery 831 on Front Street in Columbus, and it highlighted many of the local artists that were inspired by the resurgence of Tiki culture. DJ Trader Jeff spun exotica music at the show's opening reception. Columbus is also home to Mahana Productions, a Polynesian dance troupe run by Xitlali Moore that performs in central Ohio. Their goal is to spread love and appreciation for Polynesian culture. As of January 2019, a new Tiki bar opened in Powell, Ohio, called the Huli Huli Tiki Lounge and Grill. Owner Dustin Sun has high hopes for the modern and sleek-looking Tiki bar that serves classic cocktails from the recipes of Jeff "Beachbum" Berry along with a few original creations too. With an impressive cocktail menu and a five-foot-tall Moai protecting the back door, they're off to a good start.

PALM GARDEN (1934)

1298-1392 North High Street, Columbus, Ohio

This pre-Tiki night club opened on February 1, 1934, shortly after the end of Prohibition. It was created by the Lazarus department store and located downtown at 1298 North High Street. Eventually, the restaurant moved down the street to 1392 North High Street. The business was run by Joe Alexander, a prominent Columbus Italian who also owned the Desert Inn and Little Italy restaurant. The Palm Garden was a hot spot for music, drinking and dancing, and its drink menu featured tropical cocktails like the Planters Punch, Singapore Sling, Green Alligator and Zombie. The Palm Garden's menu offered a standard fare of steaks, fish, chicken and spaghetti. It also had sandwich specials for lunch. The Palm Garden hosted nationally known entertainers, including Louis Armstrong, Mel Torme, Stan Kenton and Count Basie. A young Dean Martin from Steubenville, Ohio, is also rumored to have played here. Local acts like the Noveliers, Jean March and Johnny "Rubber-Face" Frisco also got their start here. While no closing date can be found, the Palm Garden was still advertising in 1952, the same year that Tony Bennett performed there.

Left: The Pre-Tiki menu from the Palm Garden in Columbus, Ohio, circa 1940s. *Author's collection*.

Right: Who wouldn't want to see Johnny "Rubber-Face" Frisco at the Palm Garden in Columbus, Ohio? *Author's collection*.

THE GRASS SHACK AND KAHIKI SUPPER CLUB (1959–2000)

3583 East Broad Street, Columbus, Ohio

The Grass Shack was opened in 1959 by Bill Sapp and Lee Henry, and it was the first real Tiki bar in Columbus. The small building covered in thatch would inadvertently be the testing ground for the famous Kahiki Supper Club. It was the place where head Kahiki bartender Sandro Conti came up with all of the future restaurant's drink recipes. When the Grass Shack mysteriously burned down on Bill Sapp's birthday, the planning stages for one of the grandest Polynesian restaurants in the world began. Bill Sapp and Lee Henry officially opened the Kahiki Supper Club in February 1961. For almost forty years, the

The interior of the Grass Shack, or as a friend referred to it, "The Seed of the Kahiki." *Courtesy of Linda Sapp-Long.*

Kahiki was the go-to place for any celebration. Despite the building being on the National Register of Historic Places, the property was sold by Michael Tsao to the Walgreens drugstore chain, which promptly razed the building. For the full history of the Kahiki, please read *Kahiki Supper Club: A Polynesian Paradise in Columbus*, available from The History Press.

TOP OF THE ISLE

Deshler Hilton Hotel, Columbus, Ohio

The Deshler Hotel was a landmark hotel located in downtown Columbus on the corner of Broad and High Streets. The historic hotel was built in 1916 by John G. Deshler. In 1953, the hotel changed its name from the Deshler-Wallick to the Deshler-Hilton. The top floor of the hotel was partially used for fine dining. One of the first well-known restaurants to occupy the space was the Sky View Restaurant, which was known for its picturesque view of the downtown skyline. In 1963, the space was transformed into the Top of the Isle, a restaurant with a South Seas motif constructed by Glenn Wisecarver and Company. A tape machine was installed to emit sounds of crashing surf, seagulls and foghorns for authenticity, a form of Polynesian *Muzak*. The inside of the restaurant wasn't overwhelmingly Tiki, but it did have a fair amount of tropical décor, including water fountains and hand-carved Tiki barstools. The restaurant's menu featured an alluring *wahine* carrying a tempting bowl of fruit on its front cover. The inside of the menu contained a picture of a Tiki and all of the delectable Polynesian delights prepared by executive chef Martin McInerney. The male staff all wore Hawaiian shirts, and the ladies wore grass skirts and sarongs. The restaurant's drink menu offered thirty-three exotic cocktails with rum as the drinks' primary ingredient. During the day, the Isle offered an all-you-can-eat luau buffet for $1.65. For entertainment, the Top of the Isle hired the Kauai Surfriders and hula dancer Momi Lani. The highlight of Lani's performance was the Tahitian Drum Dance. The Top of the Isle was the only Polynesian restaurant in Ohio to occupy the top floor of a twelve-story building.

Local drummer Joe Martin recalled:

> *This property was one of the top-of-the-line business hotels downtown. The finer hotel properties generally had themes of some sort in the 1960s*

THE *Deshler Hilton*
COLUMBUS

Left: The Deshler Hilton Hotel in Columbus, Ohio, which used the top floor for themed restaurants, including the Top of the Isle. *Author's collection.*

Below: The Top of the Isle restaurant menu offering Tiki Tidbits and Cantonese delicacies for your dining pleasure. *Author's collection.*

Aloha - From the Top of the Isle

Tiki Tidbits

BARBECUED RIBS — $1.40
Baby Spareribs in a Sweet and Sour Sauce

ISLAND GOODIES — $1.50
Batter fried Shrimp with Hot Sauce

NUGGETS OF GOLD — $1.30
Pineapple Chunks, Water Chestnuts, Chicken Livers wrapped in Bacon

MALAYAN TIDBITS — $1.65
Egg Roll, Barbecued Pork

From The Sea

BROILED PACIFIC LOBSTER TAIL — $4.25
Served on the Shell with drawn butter

DEEP FRIED JUMBO SHRIMP — $3.25
Served on Toast with Tartar Sauce
Includes Potato, Vegetable, Salad, Beverage

From The Broiler

CHAR BROILED CHOICE SIRLOIN STRIP STEAK — $5.10
Served with Onion Rings

CHAR BROILED FILET MIGNON — $5.10
Aux Champignons

BROILED HAWAIIAN HAM STEAK — $3.25

Desserts
All your entrees

FRENCH PASTRY TRAY brought to your table — .35

Cantonese Delicacies
Chicken Egg Drop Soup $.65

From Our Cantonese Oven

PORK FOO YONG — $3.25
A mixture of finely diced cooked pork — bean sprouts — water chestnuts folded into beaten eggs fried in small cakes and served with a piquant meat sauce

MOO GOO GAI PAN — $2.95
Sliced white meat of chicken sauted with bamboo shoots, snowpea pods, mushrooms and water chestnuts

GUM GAI — $3.10
Sliced breast of chicken, diced ham, black mushrooms and garden fresh vegetables

CHICKEN CANTONESE — $3.25
Breast of chicken — water chestnuts — bamboo shoots — crisp sliced celery, artfully seasoned and steamed in a rich broth

BEEF FUGI — $3.95
Sauted with shredded Chinese and garden vegetables and garnished with fried silver noodles

CHICKEN WITH ALMONDS — $2.75
Diced chicken with mushrooms, tender bamboo shoots, crisp sliced celery. All steamed together in a rich broth and sprinkled generously with whole almonds.

SHRIMP CHOW MEIN — $3.25
Crisp bean sprouts, mushrooms, finely sliced celery, diced shrimp, superbly seasoned. Served on golden brown noodles and toasted almonds.

CHICKEN — TOP OF ISLE — $2.95
White meat of chicken with water chestnuts, garden vegetables, Cubes of Hawaiian pineapple.

CHINESE FRIED RICE — $1.50

SUSU LOBSTER CURRY — $3.95
A blending of celery, mushrooms and onions with a heavy cream curry sauce

The Islander
Tender broiled pieces of Pork, Tenderloin on a Skewer with Green Pepper, Silver Skin Onion, Tomato and Sour Sauce
$3.95
Includes Potato, Rice, Vegetable, Salad, Beverage

and 1970s. The Hilton was the place to stay, along with the Christopher Inn. The property eventually started to fade a bit because of the outgrowth of the city into suburbia. The top of the building lounge and restaurant had a Polynesian theme due to the success of the Kahiki out on the East side. The theme changed quite a few times throughout the years, as they are known to do.

The hotel would change hands multiple times before eventually closing in 1969. The building was razed in 1970, and the One Columbus skyscraper stands there today.

WAIKIKI

4101 West Broad Street, Columbus, Ohio

While the Kahiki was on east side of Broad Street, the Waikiki restaurant was located on west side. The Waikiki served authentic Polynesian cuisine for lunch and dinner, and it had a cocktail menu as well. The restaurant also provided live entertainment and a banquet facility that seated up to five hundred people. Unfortunately, on April 30, 1974, a sudden grease fire from one of the fryers sent flames through the restaurant. Several diners fled when the flames suddenly appeared in the dining room. The fire also forced guests to flee their rooms in the adjacent Imperial House West Motel. The fire caused an estimated $200,000 in total damages, and the restaurant never reopened.

HU KE LAU

1939 Fountain Square Court, Columbus, Ohio

This small restaurant was located inside a strip mall on Morse Road, just east of the Northland Mall. The Hu Ke Lau's entertainment was provided by Lani Moe and his Polynesian musicians and dancers. The restaurant also served as a venue for traveling entertainers like Sam Vine, the singing hypnotist.

HULI HULI TIKI LOUNGE AND GRILL

26 West Olentangy Street, Powell, Ohio

Huli Huli, opened in January 2019, is the latest Tiki bar to open in the Columbus area. Owner Dustin Sun purchased an old antique store in downtown Powell and completely rebuilt the inside. The décor is a modern take on Tiki, and instead of the traditional kitsch, the owners opted to present clean lines and a more sophisticated Tiki experience. In an interview with columbusundeground.com, Huli Huli general manager Nate Howe said, "The Tikiphiles take it very seriously. There's a lot of history and tradition, and we're trying to bring that back. It's truly an American craft cocktail creation."

TROPICAL BISTRO (2006–2008)

3641 Fishinger Road, Hilliard, Ohio

The Tropical Bistro was a Polynesian-themed Tiki oasis tucked inside the Mill-Run shopping center in Hilliard, Ohio. The space was previously occupied by Mark Pi's China Gate, so the inside had a considerable amount of Asian décor, including two golden lions that greeted patrons at the entrance of the dining room. The restaurant was opened in 2006 by two former employees of the Kahiki, Theang Ngo and Soeng Thong. The Bistro successfully captured the spirit of the Kahiki while it also created its own unique vision of a tropical paradise. The restaurant had colorful décor, multi-leveled booths and separate rooms that could be closed off for private parties. They catered to people who longed for a magical place to escape to. There were many artifacts from the historic Kahiki scattered throughout the restaurant, including monkey pod tables, turtle shells and Tiki masks. A vast majority of the Orchids of Hawaii lights that hung from the ceiling also came from the Kahiki. Most of these items were donated by Alice Tsao, the wife of Kahiki owner Michael Tsao, who had unexpectedly passed away in 2005.

The Tropical Bistro was known for playing traditional Hawaiian music that blended well with the tropical ambiance. On weekends, the restaurant would hire Francis Llacuna to provide live entertainment and educate

Above: Owner Theang Ngo at the Tropical Bistro in Hilliard, Ohio. *Author's collection*.

Left: Deb Chenault enjoying a Smoking Eruption cocktail at the Tropical Bistro in Hilliard, Ohio. *Author's collection*.

the audience with stories and songs about old Hawaiian traditions. The drink menu at the Bistro included many of the same cocktails that were popular at the Kahiki, including the Mai Tai, the Suffering Bastard and the Mystery Bowl. The impressive menu of colorful drink libations also included the Smoking Eruption, a drink served with dry ice that would cover your table with smoke. James Teitelbaum, author of the book *Tiki Road Trip*, commented in 2006, "The Tropical Bistro is the only place within a 350-mile radius of the ground it stands on that serves a decent tropical drink."

The Tropical Bistro used the same menu graphics for their Tropical Drink Menu as the Kahiki Supper Club. *Author's collection.*

Like the Kahiki, the Bistro's dinner menu was separated into three categories, "From the East," "From the Islands" and "From the West." While the restaurant always kept popular items on the menu, like the Tahitian Mermaid, which was a beef tenderloin stuffed with crabmeat and cream cheese, they also served an assortment of freshly made sushi. The weekend buffet was legendary.

The Tropical Bistro was also home to the Feast of the Tiki Gods, an annual event hosted by the Kahiki chapter of the Fraternal Order of Moai. The feast was the first part of a two-day festival called the Hot Rod Hula Hop. The Hula Hop's were grand events that always sold out in advance. Top-notch entertainers, like the Waitiki 7 from Hawaii and Fisherman from New York, played to enthusiastic crowds who traveled from all over the United States to attend the event. It was a complete luau feast with music, cocktails, a roast suckling pig and people wearing fezzes.

At the time, the Tropical Bistro was the only Polynesian restaurant in Columbus, but unfortunately, the odd location and lack of new customers eventually took their toll. In 2008, after just two years in business, the owners called it quits. The monkey pod tables, Orchids of Hawaii lights, Tiki mugs and other items were all sold at auction.

TAI TIKI POLYNESIAN BAR AND GRILL (2015–2016)

1014 North High Street, Columbus Ohio

The Tai Tiki was located inside the old Fireproof Records building in the Short North area of Columbus. It was owned by Tai and Gail Lieu, who also own Tai's Asian Bistro. A giant wooden re-creation of the Kahiki fireplace greeted you at the restaurant's entrance. The interior had a modern, Art Deco vibe with carved Tikis strategically placed throughout the restaurant. The restaurant's dining room area also opened out into the street. The

The sleek, modern Tiki design of Tai Tiki in Columbus, Ohio. *Author's collection.*

A wooden re-creation of the Kahiki Fireplace greeted you at the entrance of Tai Tiki in Columbus, Ohio. *Author's collection.*

menu offered upscale Chinese fare with a twist. The executive chef was Rainne Tong, who was also a Kahiki veteran. The music was always entertaining and included a lively mix of jazz, Hawaiian and surf music with occasional live performances from Francis Llacuna. Unfortunately, the lackluster cocktails coupled with skyrocketing rent ultimately doomed the small restaurant. The Tai Tiki's wooden fireplace was preserved and now resides at Tai's Asian Bistro.

DRIFTWOOD STEAK HOUSE

3369 East Main Street, Columbus, Ohio

Not much is known about Driftwood Steak House aside from a matchbook that was found, which shows a large neon palm tree sign in front of a small mid-century modern building. However, the restaurant did have its fair share of legal troubles. In 1967, thieves broke into the restaurant and stole $3,000 from Driftwood's safe. In April 1973, Mark Adams, the manager of the Driftwood Steak House, was attacked and locked in the trunk of his car by two armed robbers who ambushed him as he was leaving the restaurant. In 1980, the restaurant lost its liquor license, and without the ability to sell drinks and with steep competition from the Top Steak House just down the street, the Driftwood closed its doors for good.

GRASS SKIRT TIKI ROOM (2012–2019)

105 North Grant Street, Columbus, Ohio

The Grass Skirt was the brainchild of Columbus restaurateur Elizabeth Lessner. Later owned by Carmen Owens, the Grass Skirt was one of the best Tiki bars in the state of Ohio. The décor was top-notch and included a collection of vintage Tikis, new Tikis, a handmade skull chandelier, a lava wall and various flotsam and jetsam made by the Fraternal Order of Moai. The restaurant also boasted a nice collection of Kahiki artifacts, including the large fountain called George. The fountain was able to be purchased by the Grass Skirt and the FOM because they wanted to

The Grass Skirt Tiki Room logo.
Courtesy of Carmen Owens.

save and preserve a part of Columbus Tiki history. It sat on the Grass Skirt's patio and was lovingly restored and maintained for future generations. It is not only a hand-crafted piece of art, but it is also a piece of genuine Columbus history. Unfortunately, in August 2019 the Grass Skirt closed its doors citing sky-rocketing rent in the downtown area.

In 2018, I had the opportunity to interview Carmen Owens, the owner of the Grass Skirt:

JEFF CHENAULT. Who came up with the idea of building a Tiki bar and restaurant, and why did you do it?

CARMEN OWENS. After Liz Lessner opened Betty's in 2001, and we had opened Surly Girl in 2005, there were a million ideas and concepts being thrown around—obviously, some of them happened, and there's still a few we talk about to this day. Tiki was a concept that got batted around for a long time before it happened. I kept thinking someone else would do it, so we didn't have to! But when the Edwards Company approached Liz about opening a restaurant that would anchor the newly developing Discovery District alongside Hills Market Downtown. It seemed like a natural fit to put a Tiki bar there as a sort of "destination concept," since there wasn't much else around. After Surly got off the ground, I had said that the only other concept I would do was a Tiki bar, because I just love everything that Tiki represents—the tropical theme, escapism, kitsch, a dash of absurdity, creative atmosphere, well-made drinks, all of it. And of course, as a Columbus native, I dearly missed the Kahiki and was excited to bring a little of that back to Columbus, even if on a much smaller scale.

The Grass Skirt partners are Elizabeth Lessner, Tim Lessner, Harold Larue, Carmen Owens and Archie Brennick. All partners are still involved as of today, but they all have little to nothing to do with operations, except for me. We are all friends who go back almost twenty-five years in some cases, so we're still on great terms. We are just doing different things with our lives, and I'm a little bit of a control freak. I have always been the managing partner and, as of a few years ago, the majority owner.

JEFF. Who was involved with the construction and décor?

CARMEN. We took over the old Mad Lab space, so the building started as basically a black box, which was the first time the Columbus Food League had done a complete from-the-ground-up design of a restaurant. We used Sullivan Construction Builders, which we'd used on various projects at the other restaurants and trusted to put together a good product. As the lead on the project, I had asked my partners if we needed to hire a consultant, and they basically said, "Nah, you're smart. You know restaurants, and we trust you—go for it." We didn't have the budget for a fancy consultant anyway, so we winged it! Archie Brennick and I worked together on developing the color palette, visuals, interior and graphic design elements, as well as putting in a lot of hands-on time with the initial construction and decoration and getting things running once we opened. Archie's dad built and installed the back bar and helped with carpentry and projects all over the joint. Lara Ranallo helped with the overall design as well, especially in the kitchen. We ended up with the most badass walk-in freezer that most industry people have ever seen with her help. It's still one of my favorite things to show off behind the scenes! There's a door behind the bar with easy access to bar supplies, and the rest of the freezer is filled with food with a door to the kitchen on the other end. You can walk into the freezer from the kitchen and pop out behind the bar. No stacking syrups on top of twelve-gallon food containers on top of kegs, which is unheard of in most little restaurants! We even busted out the side of the building to fit the walk-in freezer, so we didn't have to sacrifice more interior space. Bryan Grey and Barb Baronski did the logo and graphic design elements. The bar I designed, because I wanted something that felt organic and curvy, and I even laid all the shells and glass into the resin countertop myself when the construction guys poured it. The lower, second level of that bar (the turquoise part) was retrofitted after we realized that I didn't account for enough hangover for guests to be able to eat and drink at the bar—it was like three inches of overhang, so they would have had to put everything on their laps, essentially. We initially tried a wood-epoxy-rope version that ended up being the base for the concrete that eventually got poured after the epoxy didn't cure and was a huge sticky disaster. But it was a super happy accident, because it's one of my favorite features now—guests have a functional place to eat and drink, and we have a ton of room for all the Tiki accoutrements we need to make the drinks!

After construction was mostly finished and it was time to decorate, we only had $40,000 to outfit the entire place, from paint to décor to

The skull chandelier at the Grass Skirt Tiki Bar was built by Lena Simonian and Eric Immelt. *Author's collection.*

kitchen and bar equipment, chairs/tables, et cetera. But we were fortunate to have had an army of family members and friends who came to help with everything from painting and designing to installing wallpaper, putting together tables, et cetera. A lot of days, we would just put out a call on Facebook and tell people we'd feed them and give them booze to help with whatever project needed attention that day. Lelia Cady, Wally Himelstein, my parents, the Lessner family, Archie's family, Bryan Grey, Barb Baronski and her parents—everyone from our lawyer to our regulars from the other bars—and, of course, the Fraternal Order of Moai—especially Kuku Ahu, Lena Simonian, Jimmy and Elise Robinson, Donald Drennan, Brian Panzo—and many more, were all instrumental in helping with everything from menu development to installing the matting, hanging the thatch on the walls and installing all the Tikis!

Obviously, the FOM was involved from the minute they heard there was a Tiki concept coming to Columbus, so they were a tremendous help with everything from making all of our Tiki lamps (Lena) and carving Tikis and wall hangings (Jimmy) to making any kind of décor we—or they—could think of (Donald). We all did a lot of work on the menu development together (read: drank a bunch of different versions of things after working on the bar at night), but Matt and I narrowed down the drink menu and worked out final recipes together. There were a lot of brainstorming sessions with FOM and Grass Skirt partners about how to make the lava wall happen. Harold was friends with artist Nikos Rutkowski, who refined our ideas from something abstract into a much more effective concept. (We were going to do big concrete mountains that I'm sure would have fallen on some poor guest's head at some point!) My dad built a fountain by the front door, but we ended up turning it off forever when it kept flooding the dining room floor. Oh well! It's still there by the door just looking like a bunch of tropical foliage, but it makes me happy to have a "family heirloom" there so to speak.

JEFF. Where did that large vintage Tiki in the dining room come from?

CARMEN. My mom had rented a beach house for our family in Myrtle Beach, South Carolina, the summer before we opened, so I drove down there with my whole family hoping to score some cool décor to bring back. There was so much to choose from in terms of antique shops and beach-related stores, so we bopped around all week looking for décor. We found a place called Vintiques that was amazing. They had a huge selection of vintage stuff that I combed through for hours, but of course, that Tiki was the biggest and best thing in there to my eyes. I even sent pictures back to all the partners, and Diana Lessner, Liz's mom, offered to buy it for us as a "housewarming" present. I bought some floats and nets and a large assortment of nautical stuff there as well. There was so much stuff that I had to rent my own minivan to drive it all back to Columbus!

Most of the other Tikis in the restaurant were made by Jim Robinson, also known as Chisel Slinger, in 2012. There was a huge storm that came through that summer and knocked down trees everywhere, and Jimmy said if we could get some wood to him, he would carve them for us. So, the Tikis by the door (other than the one I brought back), the big one in the hallway and many of the carvings were made by Jimmy. The owner of the Blue Danube gave us a four-inch-tall Tiki from Hawaii for an opening present as well.

JEFF. Tell us the story of acquiring the fountain George.

CARMEN. The Kahiki frozen foods company decided to get rid of the last bits of remaining Tiki décor they had a few years ago. I'm pretty sure it was a remodel of the front lobby that spurred it,

An original Tiki hand carved by Jimmy Robinson, also known as Chisel Slinger, could be seen at the Grass Skirt Tiki Bar in Columbus, Ohio. *Author's collection.*

because George was front and center when you walked into the Kahiki offices off Interstate 270. There was an online auction to sell a huge variety of things, but George was the crown jewel of the collection. The FOM offered to buy him if we would display him, and of course, we enthusiastically agreed. The night of the auction's end, we set up *three computers on the Grass Skirt bar; Archie Brennick, Kuku Ahu and I each had one. The FOM had a budget of $3,000 to start, and as it got near the end, we were close to going over budget. We agreed to pitch in another $300 and then another $200 or whatever it took to add to the FOM fund—we were all frantically refreshing our screens and screaming and panicking. Then, at the last minute, we won! It was such a celebratory night for us here. A bunch of the FOM got other stuff from the auction—there were some great Tikis and original glassware and all kinds of treasures for Tikiphiles in there—but we were dead set on George, and we got him! Fortunately, a mutual friend of ours and Grass Skirt regular, Becky, owned a funeral home at the time, so she offered the use of her crane to get him onto the patio. The installation was one of the most nail-biting times we had here, with all the FOM and Grass Skirt team helping to guide him onto the concrete pad we poured. But now he's here! And it's such a great marriage of old and new Columbus Tiki. We couldn't be more honored to house him on our patio, which was the only option since our little bar is too small to put him inside like he was at the Kahiki.*

JEFF. Who is the artist that designed the Grass Skirt art print?

CARMEN. Clinton Reno designed that for us a surprise opening gift. He had done some screen prints for Surly (and maybe the other places, but I'm not sure) and just showed up with them, numbered and signed, out of nowhere. It was such a fun interpretation too! We were so lucky that so many people in the community were excited about Tiki and willing to pitch in however they could.

JEFF. What food do you currently make in house?

CARMEN. We make our own crab rangoon, coconut shrimp, crab cakes, hush puppies, soups, desserts, salad dressings, sauces, jerk chicken, pulled pork, salsa, guacamole, queso, crab dip, veggie sausage and gravy. For drinks, we make our own simple syrup, orgeat, pomegranate grenadine, zombie mix, house-infused pineapple-coffee, pineapple-pepper and toasted coconut rum.

JEFF. Have you seen more interest in craft cocktails? What's the most popular cocktail you sell?

CARMEN. Initially, our most popular drink was the Mai Tai, but as soon as we put a Painkiller on the menu, it took top billing and stayed there. The Mai Tai and Blue Hawaiian are basically tied for the second spot, but it's my personal mission to get everyone who comes in to try a Port Light! [A] Kahiki classic, the rare bourbon tiki drink and passion fruit are exotic enough that you feel instantly transported to somewhere else.

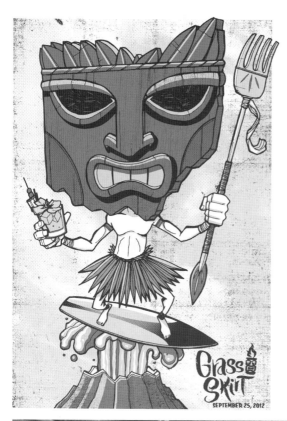

Left: This spectacular Grass Skirt Tiki Bar poster, made by artist Clinton Reno, captures the true spirit of Ohio Tiki. *Courtesy of Clinton Reno*.

Below: Interior of the Grass Skirt with bartender extraordinaire Justin Isbell. *Courtesy of Brock Ailes*.

JEFF. *How important is the music in a Tiki bar?*

CARMEN. *Music is crucial for a Tiki bar! It doesn't feel completely Tiki without the right music—like a Tiki drink without a garnish. You were a huge help in developing our "ears" for the Tiki sound. It took us a while to dial in the right mix for us in terms of tempo and vibe, but it's been fun to learn about and experiment with along the way. My favorite mix for busy times is fairly surf heavy, because it's so upbeat and it keeps the energy in the room high. But we love to play around with everything from the Beach Boys and Harry Belafonte to Amadou & Mariam. Fun fact: "Jump in the Line" has always been one of my favorite songs in the world, and now, I love even more that it puts a smile on peoples' faces every time it comes on while they're sipping a Mai Tai at the bar.*

JEFF. *Is the Hula Hop an event you look forward to?*

CARMEN. *Absolutely! The Hula Hop, in its current form, feels like the best arrangement so far, and it only keeps getting bigger each year. Initially, it was a more formal ticketed event with two five-course sit-down dinners with Francis Llacuna (an original Hawaiian entertainer that I adore) as the indoor entertainment, and the Grass Skirt parking lot was used for bands and drinks outside. But as the crowd got bigger and we got more established, it made more sense to move the party to a bigger space outside, so we took over both our lot and the corner lot next to it. The current arrangement allows the Hula Hop to be a huge outdoor party and raise funds for Cure CMD, a nonprofit organization dedicated to curing congenital muscular dystrophy. It also allows the Grass Skirt to maintain its usual atmosphere inside, so we can accommodate regular guests as well as the Hula Hoppers. It's phenomenal as a showcase for bands and Tiki vendors from all over. It's also a great way to introduce new people to the Grass Skirt who may have never been here before. And all the while, we're raising money for a great cause, so it's a party with a purpose, which feels great to be a part of.*

JEFF. *What do you think of the resurgence of Polynesian culture?*

CARMEN. *First off, I'm thrilled that Tiki bars are coming back as an arm of the craft cocktail movement and that people are taking it seriously on both sides of the bar. And I say, the more, the merrier! We only opened the Grass Skirt because no one else had brought Tiki back to Columbus yet, we wanted it to be here and we had the opportunity and made it happen. With a budget of $40,000 after construction to decorate and equip the whole place, we definitely came on the scene as the smallest of small businesses. So, I love to see what people do with other resources and different spaces*

A Hot Rod Hula Hop postcard that features the Supersuckers, Coffin Daggers and Vegas 66. The Supersuckers played on top of a bowling alley inside the Sequoia Pro Bowl in Columbus. *Author's collection.*

everywhere I go. I love to travel and see what old-school gems I've missed and the new stuff that's come up since I visited last.

As a drinker and a bar owner, Tiki has always been my favorite way to experience—and to be a part of—craft cocktail culture. In a lot of ways, Surly Girl Saloon felt like a "proto" Tiki bar to me. It was an immersive environment that was a mashup of the bordello, pirate and cowgirl cultures that we just made up ourselves and populated with the food and drinks that were inspired by the bizarre theme. Getting into Tiki from both the consumer and producer side was a wonderful opportunity to stretch my brain and palette to new places. There's endless opportunity for education, exploration and development, and I also love that Tiki always presents fun rather than being so serious. That's just the part of me that loves kitsch, absurdism, surrealism and escapism in any forms that I can find them. If

I could convince Paul Reubens to let me open a Pee Wee's Playhouse bar, I'd do it in a heartbeat! I love that Tiki fits exactly into that part of my wheelhouse, and that's why Grass Skirt will always have more of a surf shack vibe than a neo-Tiki modernist take on the genre.

I think we're in an interesting moment with cultural appropriation as a legitimate concern in the world of Tiki. In part, that's why we stopped offering plastic leis at the door here. As a bar owner with an anthropology degree, it was part of the discussion as we created the concept, and it still is an ongoing conversation behind the scenes. I think we're trying to be respectful of where things are coming from and pay homage to a multitude of cultures in a way that I hope comes across as playful but not like putting on a costume. It's South Pacific–inspired décor, Caribbean inspired-drinks and coastal-inspired food. To me, it feels like Tiki is a made-up culture rather than a stolen culture, because there's no one place to point to and say, "That's what we're trying to be." The only actual reference to what Tiki bars are doing are other Tiki bars, and those have opened in the tropical places they were inspired by. An authentic Hawaiian Mai Tai is basically unrecognizable to a Tikiphile as a true Mai Tai. To me, that's the biggest trip of the whole movement! Like, Hawaii, you don't need a Tiki bar— you're freaking Hawaii!

The drink menu at the Grass Skirt was impressive, with two different versions of the Mai Tai, two versions of the Zombie and a signature cocktail called Ahu's Navy Grog #2. This drink is the original creation of founding FOM member and mixologist Kuku Ahu.

Ahu's Navy Grog

¾ ounce fresh lime juice
¾ ounce grapefruit juice
¾ ounce Grade A maple syrup
½ ounce Fernet Branca
2 dashes Fee Brothers Old Fashion Aromatic Bitters
2 ounces Appleton Estate 12-Year Rum

Shake well with ice, pour into your favorite cocktail glass. Garnish with a lime slice and fresh mint.

Recipe courtesy of Kuku Ahu and Grass Skirt Tiki Room.

THE HISTORY OF GEORGE

The Kahiki fountain (also known as George) is one of the last remaining sculptures from the famed Kahiki Supper Club. The Kahiki was an iconic restaurant that was listed in the National Register of Historic Places and was recognized as the largest and best-preserved Polynesian restaurant in the United States. As such, the artifacts it contained were just as important. The Kahiki fountain was built by Philip E. Kientz in 1960, and it was placed in the center of the foyer to greet customers and serve as the "Guardian of the Quiet Village." Water would flow from the top of George's head, out of

George is a well-preserved Kahiki artifact that most recently could be seen at the Grass Skirt Tiki Bar in Columbus, Ohio. *Author's collection.*

his mouth and down around his body. As the water collects in the basin, it is recirculated throughout the hollow statue. George was also illuminated from the inside, and fog would periodically engulf him. To many visitors, George was a sight to behold. The fountain was designed by Coburn Morgan, a famous interior designer responsible for many of the restaurant's unique decorations, including the famous Moai statues and the Tiki fireplace. Coburn Morgan also designed a lot of other themed restaurants, including the Wine Cellar (Columbus), the Thunderbird Restaurant (Lima) and the Tangier (Akron). The Kahiki fountain represents a significant period in the development of the themed restaurant industry and is a remarkably intact example of Polynesian Pop architecture.

OTHER COLUMBUS TIKI RESTAURANTS

Beachcomber Lounge
37 West State Street, Columbus, Ohio

The Castaways Bar and Grill
153 East Gay Street, Columbus, Ohio

The Castaways Lounge
3911 Sullivant Avenue, Columbus, Ohio

2

CINCINNATI

Cincinnati was destined to be a city that loved Tiki culture. When Hawaii became a state in 1959, the Cinerama film *South Sea Adventure* was making the rounds and played to enthusiastic crowds at the Capitol Theatre. In 1960, the Mall at Swifton Center honored servicemen of the U.S. Navy for an entire weekend by having a Hula Holiday. For three nights, guests could taste the exotic delights of an authentic Hawaiian luau while listening to the soft tropical sounds of Bob "Pulevai" Waters and the Paradise Islanders. In 1964, Bob and his group started their career at the Howard Johnson's Motor Lodge and Hawaiian Village, which lasted for an unprecedented twenty years. In 1965, Stephen Crane opened the Kon-Tiki restaurant inside downtown Cincinnati's Sheraton-Gibson Hotel. Shortly thereafter, the city exploded with other Polynesian restaurants hoping to jump in on the tropical trend. Hawaiian-themed dances, dinner proms and company parties proliferated throughout the 1960s and 1970s. The local Holiday Inns had luaus every weekend. In 1971, the Netherland Hilton Hotel's Palm Court transformed into a Hawaiian luau every Saturday night. For $6.95 per person, guests could indulge in a "no limit" cocktail hour beginning at 7:00 p.m., which featured exotic drinks and an all-you-can-eat Hawaiian buffet featuring roast suckling pig, teriyaki steak, chicken bula bula, lomi lomi salmon, haupia and poi. From 9:00 p.m. to 10:00 p.m., the Netherland had a floor show featuring the Aloha Hawaiians with native music, hula dancing and island folklore. Bill Sapp was even approached about opening a Kahiki in Cincinnati, but unfortunately, the planned restaurant never panned out. Cincinnati is also

Netherland Hilton

CINCINNATI

Left: The Netherland Hilton Hotel is a historic hotel in downtown Cincinnati. *Author's collection*.

Below: An advertisement for the Hawaiian Luau at the Netherland Hilton Palm Court. Rumor has it that, at times, you could indulge in a "no limit" cocktail hour. *Author's collection*.

HAWAIIAN LUAU

EVERY SATURDAY NIGHT

AT THE
NETHERLAND HILTON PALM COURT

Deluxe Luau Dinner (ALL YOU CAN EAT) ala carte Portions Available

$**6**⁹⁵

per person (plus tax & gratuity)

Floor Show Featuring Famous "Aloha Hawaiians" 2 Shows Nightly, 7 and 10:00

PLEASE CALL FOR RESERVATION: 621-3800

LIMITED SEATING ONLY

FREE PARKING: 123 WEST 6TH ST.. PARKADE GARAGE

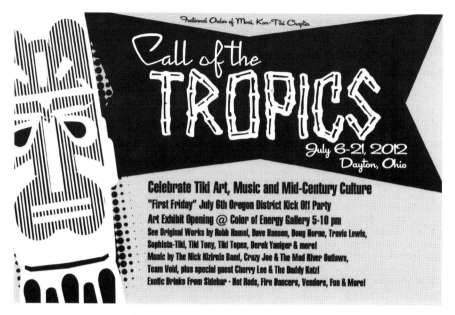

The Call of the Tropics was a unique Tiki art show curated by the Kon Tiki Chapter of the Fraternal Order of Moai. *Courtesy of Dave Larsen.*

home to the Kon-Tiki chapter of the Fraternal Order of Moai. Over the years, the Fraternal Order of Moai has had multiple Tiki-themed events, including Festiki in 2010, which was sponsored by Surf Ohio, and Call of the Tropics in 2012, a Tiki-themed art show in nearby Dayton. With all of Cincinnati's rich Polynesian background, it's sad to report that there are currently no Tiki bars in the city.

THE PATIO RESTAURANT

Netherland Hilton, Lower Arcade, Carew Tower, Cincinnati, Ohio

The Carew Tower is a beautifully historic forty-nine-story French Art Deco building in downtown Cincinnati that was completed in 1931. The Netherland Plaza Hotel was part of the Tower and centrally located within blocks of additional shops and fine dining. The landmark hotel was one of the first multiuse complexes in the United States that offered an office tower, hotel, automated garage, various shops and multiple restaurants.

According to the Historic Hotels of America website:

The historic hotel's main lobby and mezzanine areas feature a half acre of rare Brazilian rosewood, extensive use of German silver, and a stylized Egyptian décor reinforced with delicate floral motifs. There are also exquisitely detailed frescoes, ceiling murals, an original Rookwood fountain with a pair of matching seahorses, and the refined Restaurants at Palm Court, which includes Orchids at Palm Court—named #7 Best Restaurant in the USA by OpenTable in 2014.

When the hotel originally opened in 1931, it had a total of seven restaurants: the Frontier Room, the Restaurant Continentale, the Arcadia Tea Room, the Coffee Shop, the Rotisserie Grill, the Luncheonette and the Pavillion Caprice. The Pavillion Caprice was a "big band" nightclub that featured live entertainment. It was designed by New York decorator Jac Lessman. Jac also redesigned the Old Vienna restaurant, a restaurant and beer garden beneath the Carew Tower, which later reopened as the Patio Restaurant. When the Patio opened in 1941, it was Cincinnati's newest dine-and-dance emporium. The Vine Street entrance, along with the stairwell, which descended from it, was eliminated. They also moved the orchestra stand from the west side of the room to the east side. The four pillars, which used to surround the dance floor, were disguised as overstuffed pineapples. Hawaiian rattan chairs were also used to furnish the rest of the room. Paul Penny was the manager, and the restaurant featured a Latin American revue twice a night. Don Juan Rodrigo's six-piece rumba band provided the music for dancers Lola and Andre and their troupe. The Patio launched to a sellout crowd.

STEPHEN CRANE

Steve Crane was a Hollywood actor and restaurateur. So much has happened in Steve's career that you could write a book on just his glamourous Hollywood escapades. However, this book will focus on his restaurant business. Crane's first restaurant was Lucey's, a favorite of the movie colony in 1943. As a former actor, now a restaurant host and owner, Crane became a well-known name. He even helped Don the Beachcomber open his own restaurant in Honolulu in 1947. Struck by the Polynesian

Overlooking
Fountain Square

SHERATON-GIBSON

The Sheraton-Gibson Hotel was home to Stephen Crane's Kon Tiki restaurant in Cincinnati, Ohio. *Author's collection.*

bug, Crane purchased the Tropics restaurant in Beverly Hills in 1953 and renamed it the Luau. The Luau was known for its tropical décor and finely crafted cocktails. The Hawaiian craze in California was booming and so was Crane's restaurant business. In 1958, Crane expanded his company and founded Stephen Crane Associates. While Trader Vic's had partnered with the Hilton Hotel Chain, an opportunity arose, thanks to Skipper Kent, to place Polynesian restaurants inside Sheraton Hotels across the country. Stephan Crane Associates jumped on the opportunity and partnered with Sheraton Hotels to build the Kon-Tiki restaurants. Together, they built locations in Montreal, Portland, Chicago, Cincinnati, Cleveland, Honolulu and Boston. Steve also operated a couple of smaller restaurants called Port O' Call in both Dallas and Toronto. Gabe Florian

Above: The Tiki Bowl was a popular drink at the Stephen Crane's Kon Tiki restaurants. Today, the bowls are highly collectible. *Courtesy of Scott Schell*.

Right: Actor, ladies' man and restaurateur Stephen Crane enjoying a Scorpion Bowl at the Kon Tiki. *Courtesy of Scott Schell*.

Steve's Rum Barrel was introduced to the Kon Tiki menu in 1961, and it has been a hit with sophisticated savages ever since. *Courtesy of Scott Schell.*

was hired as the art director and designer for Stephen Crane and Associates. Together with George Nakashima, who had previously worked for architect of the Beverly Hilton Welton Becket, they would go on to design the entire chain of Kon-Tiki restaurants. Like Trader Vic's, Crane had his own unique Tiki mugs and bowls, and today, they are highly prized collector's items. The Luau and Kon-Tiki restaurants flourished and remained popular throughout the 1960s and 1970s. By the late 1970s, however, Polynesian restaurants were in decline, and Tiki was considered tacky. In 1978, Crane sold the Luau for over $4 million and promptly retired. He successfully cashed in on America's Tiki craze for twenty-five years and had fun doing it. Crane passed away in 1985, but the legacy of his Polynesian-themed Tiki bars still resonates today. It's also interesting to note that Ohio was the only state to host two Kon-Tiki restaurants.

KON-TIKI AT THE SHERATON-GIBSON HOTEL

421 Walnut Street, Cincinnati, Ohio

This was the fourth Kon-Tiki Restaurant to be built in partnership with the Sheraton-Gibson Hotel and Stephen Crane Associates. The other Kon-Tikis were located in Montreal, Portland and Cleveland. Before the $125,000 renovation of the space, it was occupied by the famous Florentine Room, an elegant Italian restaurant. The marbled columns and paneled architecture were replaced with a bamboo-braced roof and tropical décor. For Crane, the Kon-Tiki restaurant in Cincinnati was an economy model. It was much smaller in size and shared its kitchen with the hotel. This location also lacked some of the tropical pools, waterfalls and an abundance of décor that the larger locations had. Still, the multicolored light fixtures made from fish floats, rattan fish traps and ancient baskets provided the space with unique lighting and perfectly complemented the jungle ambience. The wall decorations included paddles, ancient wooden weapons and other paraphernalia from the islands. The Kon-Tiki officially opened on August 23, 1965. The Polynesian restaurant, at the time, complemented the hotel's other themed restaurant Yeatman's Cove, which was nautical in design. Despite all the hoopla and advertising, the restaurant was never successful in Cincinnati. Eventually, the entire contents of the Kon-Tiki were sold at auction for $15,000, and the space was converted back into an Italian restaurant.

Luau Fried Shrimp

2 pounds raw shrimp (size 16–20 per pound)
1 cup flour, sifted
1 cup cornstarch
½ teaspoon salt
½ teaspoon baking powder
1 teaspoon catsup
Water

Remove shells from shrimp and butterfly from back to tail. Wash out sand vein and dry thoroughly. For batter, blend remaining ingredients, adding enough water to make batter consistency of pancake batter. Dip shrimp in batter. Shake off excess batter. Deep fry in oil heated to 375 degrees until crisp and brown. Makes four servings.

HOWARD JOHNSON'S MOTOR LODGE AND HAWAIIAN VILLAGE

11440 Chester Road, Sharonville, Ohio

By 1965, Howard Johnson had come a long way from opening an ice cream stand in 1926 to building a coast-to-coast chain of restaurants and motor lodges. Johnson's restaurants had one of the first reservation systems in the country, and the waitress uniforms were designed by Christian Dior. The

DINE . . . DANCE
SATURDAY NIGHTS
NINE 'TIL ONE
at the
HAWAiiAN ViLLAGE
featuring the popular
PARADISE ISLANDERS
AUTHENTIC
POLYNESIAN FOOD and MUSIC
"LUAU AT POOLSIDE"
ONLY $3.75 from 6:00 to 8:00
Reservations Suggested
Call 771-3400
HOWARD JOHNSON'S
SHARON ROAD EXIT OFF I-75

For twenty years, the Luau at Howard Johnson's Hawaiian Village reigned supreme in the food and entertainment industry in Cincinnati. *Author's collection.*

Howard Johnson's brand of frozen food was even available in grocery stores. On April 18, 1964, Howard Johnson's Motor Lodge and Hawaiian Village opened in Sharonville, a suburb of Cincinnati. The "Burst of Orange Splendor" was located on a twenty-three-acre site on Chester Road right off the Interstate 75 exit. At the time, the ultra-modern $2 million lodge was the largest franchised motor lodge in the chain, with two stories and 150 rooms. For honeymooners, the lodge had the Garden Suite, for business executives it had the Granada and Barcelona Suites and for an escape to the South Seas, it had the Hawaiian Village. Homer Shrewsbury was the designer of the Hawaiian Village. While the main building resembled most Howard Johnson lodges throughout the country, this location served as a showcase for Shrewbury's talent. The lodge included a complete Hawaiian Village with an indoor swimming pool encircled by a lounge, faux palm trees, artificial foliage, flowing streams and waterfalls. The lodge also had a thatch-roofed beverage bar called the Mai-Tai Hut. There was an adjoining steam room, sunroom and children's play area called the Wee-Lani. Homer Shrewsbury's designing credits also include the refurbished Everglades Hotel in Miami and a jet-age air terminal in the Grand Bahamas.

The lodge's Hawaiian luaus were so successful that the company built two additional wings to the Hawaiian Village, a new kitchen on the south side and a swim club on the north. To enhance the tropical experience, on October 24, 1964, the lodge hired Bob "Pulevai" Waters and his Paradise Islanders for a three-week contract to provide entertainment for the big Saturday-night luaus. The Paradise Islanders were a group of performers formed by Sam Koki, who regularly played in Honolulu and Hollywood. Sam gave Waters permission to use the Paradise Islanders' name, and the rest is history. Bob became well known and respected in Hawaiian music circles and continued to play at the Hawaiian Village on and off for the next twenty years. Bob eventually retired from the Paradise Islanders in 1986. According to Dan Clare, "The musical legacy Bob Waters left was unique. He established, nurtured and propagated the Hawaiian entertainment tradition in the Cincinnati area for many years. Even after Bob retired, his band continued to perform, helping to seal his musical legacy."

The Howard Johnson's Hawaiian Village continued to perform its famous luaus in the 1980s, but they eventually faded into obscurity. In 1988, the Marriott Corporation bought Howard Johnson's for $314 million. The main building is currently a Marriott Fairfield Inn and Suites. The last Howard Johnson's restaurant closed in 2015.

KALI-KAI (1965–1983)

6202 Montgomery Road, Cincinnati, Ohio

Opened in 1965, the Kali-Kai was a Cantonese and Polynesian restaurant owned by William Mirman. It was originally called the Kon-Tiki, but the owners were forced to change the restaurant's name due to legal issues with the Kon-Tiki restaurant chain owned by Stephen Crane and Associates. The building at 6202 Montgomery Road was formerly the home of the Top o' the Ridge Restaurant. Mirman also owned Saylor's Port, a famous floating river restaurant that was built on a converted sugar barge. The Kali-Kai was moderately decorated with bamboo and wall decorations, but it was the Mirman's food and drinks that brought in his loyal customers. The restaurant's executive chef was Sonny Mah, whose specialty was an original dish called Chicken Velvet. It consisted of lightly fried chicken breast with almonds and Asian vegetables covered with an exquisite

Left: An early advertisement for the Kon-Tiki in Cincinnati. The name was later changed to Kali-Kai to avoid a lawsuit from Stephen Crane, who owned the rights to the Kon-Tiki name. *Author's collection*.

Below: An advertisement for the Kali-Kai in Cincinnati offers a Cantonese Appetizer Plate along with customers' favorite cocktails for lunch. *Author's collection*.

cream sauce; the sauce was so good its recipe was a highly guarded secret. Another favorite dish was the House of Kali-Kai Special, which consisted of fried rice, chicken, two barbecue ribs, two pieces of barbecue pork, three fried shrimp, three fried wontons and lobster meat with imported mushrooms and fresh vegetables, all for $4.95. In 1967, the restaurant moved to 3908 Reading Road and continued to have good business until eventually closing in 1983.

LUAU RESTAURANT

126 East Sixth Street, Cincinnati, Ohio

In 1965, George Smith bought the financially plagued Savory Cafeteria from a sheriff's sale and made plans to remodel it into a Polynesian restaurant. Smith was no stranger to the restaurant business; he was already the general manager for David's Buffet and Captain David's. The Hawaiian craze was just taking off in Cincinnati with the Kon-Tiki at the Sheraton-Gibson and the successful Howard Johnson's Hawaiian Village. Everyone in town was having a luau, so the name of the restaurant came naturally. It was decorated with thatch-roofed huts and plenty of bamboo. Waterfalls, coconut palms, fish nets and glass floats permeated the atmosphere. There was even a bamboo-lined doorway topped with a large dragon's head at the entrance. The restaurant was designed by Roger Barron, who worked at Hallbach's in Dayton, a restaurant supply company based in Kentucky. The restaurant's food was served buffet-style and called Mainland Feasts. The buffet table was built on top of an outrigger canoe and loaded with various American, Chinese and Polynesian foods.

TAHIKI LOUNGE

5503 Cheviot Road, Montfort Heights, Ohio

The Tahiki was originally opened by Don Schmidt in 1964. A year later, Schmidt's wife became ill, and he sold the business to Edward J. Lloyd and Raymond L. Trimble, two bail bondsmen who turned the club into a topless go-go lounge. The lounge was managed by Milt Magel, and then later by Ronnie Trimble, Ray's brother. I'm sure the tropical décor was minimal, but their matchbook did have a Tiki face on it. Over the years, they kept adding more go-go girls. By the time ten girls were working at the lounge, local advertisements were stating, "With Ten Go-Go Girls You Get Egg Rolls."

In 1966, Ed Lloyd financially backed up the singing career of Janie Fulmer. Janie started working in the lounge as a waitress and later became a featured singer in the club. She had started singing a few years earlier and was encouraged by the Ginger Lee Trio to take the spotlight. Janie's single "Wild and Free" was released on the Alco label, which was owned by Arvie Webster. Despite all of the label's efforts, including Arvie climbing to the top of the WSAL tower as a promotional stunt, the single never managed to take off.

Linda Wainscott, a go-go girl at the Tahiki, helped make a movie of the club's entertainment in 1967. Since the performers were billed as "Cincinnati's Wildest Floor Show," the film seemed only natural. The restaurant made color movies of the lounge's one dozen girls in action and loaned them for showings to other groups and business clubs. A professional NBC photographer made the film, and Johnny Carson went on to play a portion of it on the *Tonight Show* in March 1967.

By July 1969, the dancers were picketing outside for more pay. The business would eventually close a year later, but its tax problems with the IRS did not end with the business. In 1974, Judge David S. Porter of the U.S. District Court ordered the owners to pay $26,571, including interest, in back employment taxes between 1965 and 1967. The owners had falsely claimed that the dancers were independent contractors and not employees. During the court trial, several dancers testified about the unsavory work conditions and how they were required to solicit ten drinks a night from customers.

VARONE'S TROPICANA AND BAMBOO ROOM

Kenwood and Pfeiffer Roads, Cincinnati, Ohio

Varone's Tropicana and Bamboo Room opened on December 3, 1954. It was owned by husband-and-wife team Carlos and Virginia Varone. They were a famous dance team known as Don Carlos and Dolores before deciding to open a club of their own. The Bamboo Room was the show spot of the Tropicana and had a local following with star entertainment every week.

OTHER CINCINNATI TIKI RESTAURANTS

Bill the Beachcomber
4596 Paddock Road, Cincinnati, Ohio

Head Hunters
2820 Wayne Avenue, Cincinnati, Ohio

The Islander
4228 North Main Street, Cincinnati, Ohio

Mermaid Lounge (Go-go Lounge)
3100 East Third, Cincinnati, Ohio

Paradise Inn
1430 Wayne Avenue, Cincinnati, Ohio

Tradewinds (Go-go Lounge)
700 Watervliet Avenue, Cincinnati, Ohio

Outrigger Lounge
2734 Salem Avenue, Cincinnati, Ohio

3

CLEVELAND

Cleveland has a unique history in Tiki lore. In the pre-Tiki days, the city had two tropical watering holes: the Club Zombie in the Hawley House Hotel and the Bamboo Room inside the Hotel Olmstead. On a list of themed restaurants in Cleveland, you could also include Herman Pirchner's Eldorado Club Alpine Village since it was the premier downtown restaurant for theater goers from 1934 to 1961. Cleveland was also the home to the *Guitarist* magazine, which later became the Oahu Publishing Company, in the 1930s. Back then, Oahu Publishing was one of the kingpins of the Hawaiian music craze; it sold sheet music and educational tools for musicians all over the world. Its catalogue was filled with Hawaiian guitars, steel guitars and amplifiers for sale, and it held Honolulu Guitar Club meetings every week. There was a big fascination with Hawaiian music and culture in the United States at this time, and most of it emanated from Cleveland. Radio stations were playing Hawaiian music too; in the 1960s, WKYC in Cleveland broadcast a radio serial called Congo Curt. The series was written and performed by disc jockeys Harry Martin and Specs Howard. The show was about the adventures, or misadventures, of Congo Curt—think Rocky and Bullwinkle placed in a jungle setting and you'll have an idea of what it was like. The background music for this show was pure exotica and sounds suspiciously like Martin Denny. It was so popular that a Congo Curt record was released that includes eight episodes of the original serials. After the Kon-Tiki closed in 1976, Cleveland was devoid of Tiki for years. With the opening of Porco's Lounge and the Tiki Underground, the city is finally reclaiming its Tiki history.

Above: An impressive logo design for the Oahu Publishing Company in Cleveland, Ohio. *Author's collection*

Left: In the 1930s, the Oahu Publishing Company offered courses of Hawaiian guitar lessons, along with a full line of instruments, amps and teaching materials. *Author's collection*.

59

This bizarre record of Congo Curt serials was released by WKYC in Cleveland. It's a bizarre mix of jungle comedy antics and exotica music. *Author's collection.*

KON-TIKI AT THE SHERATON-CLEVELAND HOTEL

24 Public Square, Cleveland, Ohio

In the 1960s, the concept of themed specialty restaurants was embedded in the hotel industry. The Hilton chain had Trader Vic's, the Marriott had the Kona Kai and the Sheraton had the Kon-Tiki. The Kon-Tiki located in the Sheraton-Cleveland Hotel operated from 1961 to 1976. This was the third Kon-Tiki restaurant built in partnership with the Sheraton Hotels following the Montreal and Portland locations. According to Stephen S.J. Hall, the decision to build the Kon-Tiki in Cleveland was a big one. The city had a reputation of having been deserted for the suburbs. Except for a few popular downtown spots, the city's evening food and beverage business was falling. The decision to build the Kon-Tiki in Cleveland was ultimately a good one; the chain of restaurants became known for its elaborate décor, excellent service and detailed tableware and dinnerware. Stephen Crane and Associates spent a lot more money on décor at the Cleveland location than they did in Cincinnati. Each dining room had a different tropical theme or region. Between the Tepe and Patio Rooms were carved Tiki poles and a bridge over a lava rock pool and waterfall. The serpentine bar in the Aikane Room had a waterfall in the background; it also had a thatched roof with blowfish lamps hanging over the bar. The Patio Room was covered in a jungle of exotic plants and included a waterfall that emanated from a giant clam shell on the wall. Even the Maori Long Hut featured a native outrigger canoe suspended from the ceiling. The Maori weapons and shields displayed on the split-bamboo walls gave the room an authentic "meetinghouse" look. Stephen Crane's restaurants were immensely popular and iconic symbols of America's love affair with Polynesia

Three ladies hanging out with the three cannibal Tikis outside of the Kon-Tiki Restaurant at the Sheraton-Cleveland Hotel. *Courtesy of Scott Schell.*

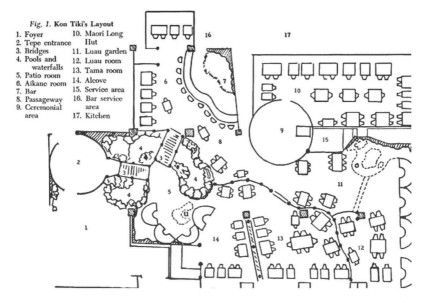

Fig. 1. Kon Tiki's Layout
1. Foyer
2. Tepe entrance
3. Bridges
4. Pools and waterfalls
5. Patio room
6. Aikane room
7. Bar
8. Passageway
9. Ceremonial area
10. Maori Long Hut
11. Luau garden
12. Luau room
13. Tama room
14. Alcove
15. Service area
16. Bar service area
17. Kitchen

A blueprint of the interior of the Kon-Tiki at the Sheraton-Cleveland Hotel shows all of the various rooms, pools, bridges and waterfalls in the restaurant. *Author's collection.*

A beautiful look inside the Kon-Tiki Restaurant at the Sheraton-Cleveland Hotel. *Courtesy of Scott Schell.*

The War God Tiki mug was available exclusively at Stephen Crane's Kon-Tiki Restaurants. *Courtesy of Scott Schell.*

during the 1950s and 1960s. By the 1970s, the Tiki theme was in decline, and in 1976, the Kon-Tiki closed its doors for good. The space is currently occupied by the Cleveland Renaissance Hotel and is rumored to have a few of the carved Tikis still on the grounds.

War God

½ ounce fresh lime juice
½ ounce grapefruit juice
½ ounce Falernum syrup
¼ ounce sugar syrup
1 ounce Virgin Islands rum
1 ounce dark Jamaican rum
1 ounce 151-proof Demerara rum
6 drops (about ⅛ teaspoon) Herb Saint or Pernod
Dash of Angostura Bitters
8 ounces (1 cup) crushed ice

Put everything in a blender, saving ice for last. Blend at high speed for no more than five seconds. Pour into a War God mug, adding more ice to fill.

Recipe from the Stephen Crane's Kon-Tiki restaurant, courtesy of Jeff "Beachbum" Berry.

PACIFIC PEARL

4620 Richmond Road, Cleveland, Ohio

At the opening of the Pacific Pearl, advertisements exclaimed, "Hawaii is only a short drive from Akron." The Pacific Pearl was located inside the Plaza Square in Warrensville Heights, a suburb of Cleveland. Among the flamboyant décor, the restaurant served plenty of Mai Tais to go along with its island cooking. It's unclear how much décor was in this place, but it did have its own floor show. The star attraction was Chief Mapu and his Hawaiian family. The group performed traditional dances in authentic costumes from Tahiti, New Zealand, Samoa, Fiji, Tonga and Hawaii. There was a luau every night, except for Monday, complete with music, dancing and flaming swords. The weekends were so busy that the owners recommended that their guests book two weeks in advance. Now that's a luau!

THE BAMBOO ROOM

Hotel Olmstead, East Ninth at Superior, Cleveland, Ohio

The Hotel Olmstead was a popular spot for traveling businessmen and people attending the nearby Playhouse Theatre. It had three hundred rooms with a bath and radio in every room—a pretty remarkable feat back in the 1940s. The hotel had two bars to choose from: the Guild Room and the Bamboo Room. Both the bars and the coffee shop were air-conditioned, another luxury. The Bamboo Room opened in 1945 and had a South Seas atmosphere combined with an Art Deco sophistication. It had an extensive drink menu as well.

CLUB ZOMBIE

The Hawley House, West Third at St. Clair, Cleveland, Ohio

In 1882, brothers David and Davis Hawley partnered with John Langton to start the construction of the Hawley House at the corner of St. Clair

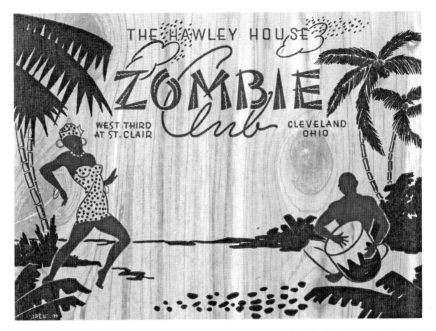

A Club Zombie Restaurant menu from the Hawley House in Cleveland, Ohio, circa the 1940s. *Courtesy of Scott Schell.*

FAMOUS TROPICAL DRINKS

"ZOMBIE"
DEFINITELY TORRID
.75

RONRICO "FRESH FRUIT" WEST INDIES COCKTAIL .50
Specify your favorite fresh fruit

HURRICANE PUNCH	.50	**KUI PAI**	.50
"Storm Warning"		"Wicky-Wacky-Woo-woo"	
SWIZZLE	.50	**RICO ROYAL**	.75
"Roll Your Own"		"Royalty In Taste"	
DOUBLE "R"	.50	**RED RUMMIE**	.50
"Sweet And Lovely"		"Picks You Up And Up And Up"	
SPARKLING RONRICO	.50	**SHARKS TOOTH**	.50
"Colorful As A Miami Night"		"The Devil Drink Of Mexico"	
VIRGIN ISLAND	.50	**PINEAPPLE WHISK**	.50
"Good For Colds — If She's Cold"		"Now Hold Tight"	
RUM COW	.50	**HOT BUTTERED RUM**	.50
"And We Don't Mean Ferdinand!"		"Youth Renewing"	

Some of the drinks available at Club Zombie included the Ronrico, the Rum Cow and, of course, the Zombie. *Courtesy of Scott Schell.*

A rare bottle of Club Zombie cologne for those who not only want to look like a zombie but smell like one, too. *Courtesy of Sven Kirsten.*

Avenue and Seneca Street. It was a four-story, one-hundred-room hotel that became one of the most popular in Cleveland. It was also a popular meeting place for various civic organizations. Another floor was added to the hotel in 1901 to accommodate its increasing business. The Club Zombie opened on December 17, 1940, and quickly became the go-to place for late-night socializing, music and tropical cocktails. The drink menu included such cocktails as the Hurricane Punch, the Virgin Island, the Sharks Tooth and the Zombie, among others.

The menu warned of the club's habit-forming potential: "If our efforts in bringing you the beauty and romance of the Tropical Islands together with an abundance of delicious food, drink and entertainment, has been successful, then we feel that we have been rewarded and that we shall see you again and again."

MICHAUD'S ALOHA RESTAURANT

4250 Pearl Road, Cleveland Ohio

In 1961, advertisements for Michaud's restaurant exclaimed, "Tropical atmosphere and cuisine featuring a Royal Hawaiian Buffet." The Hawaiian feast was served buffet-style and included island gourmet items like teriyaki beef, mahi-mahi, Royal Hawaiian fowl and a complete assortment of native Hawaiian delicacies.

PORCO'S LOUNGE AND TIKI ROOM (2013–PRESENT)

2527 West Twenty-Fifth Street, Cleveland, Ohio

Established in 2013 and still going strong, Porco's Lounge and Tiki Room is a Polynesian paradise. The lounge is owned and operated by Stefan Was and his wife, Anne-Marie, and they are keeping its Tiki torches burning bright. This exotic retreat is the first authentic Tiki bar to open in Cleveland since the Kon-Tiki closed its doors in 1976. Upon entering the building, guests are instantly transported to the Tropics. The décor has a history all its own, with memorabilia from the Kon-Tiki and other Polynesian restaurants adorning the bamboo walls and fixtures. The lounge even commissioned Danny Gallardo of Tiki Diablo to make a signature Tiki mug.

The Porco Lounge and Tiki Bar's exterior sign in Cleveland, Ohio. *Courtesy of Sam Walker.*

TIKI UNDERGROUND (2017–PRESENT)

5893 Akron-Cleveland Road, Hudson, Ohio

The Tiki Underground is one of the newest Tiki establishments to open in Ohio. The owners, Sean and Jessie Coffey, opened the 4,500-square-foot Tiki bar just outside of Cleveland in Hudson, Ohio, in 2017. Tiki Underground was an extension of Sean's home Tiki bar and his love for Polynesian culture. The lounge is decorated with bamboo walls, Tiki lamps, Witco art and a huge collection of flotsam and jetsam from the Coffeys' personal collection give the place a unique South Pacific atmosphere.

MAI KAI ROOM AT THE MIDWAY MOTEL

6455 Pearl Road, Cleveland, Ohio

The Mai Kai Room was the restaurant portion of the Midway Motel. The motel also had another room called the Tradewinds, which was used exclusively for drinking and dancing.

OTHER CLEVELAND TIKI RESTAURANTS

Aloha Kai
1252 Euclid Avenue, Cleveland, Ohio

Hurricane Room
2016 East Sixty-Fifth Street, Cleveland, Ohio

Port O' Call Supper Club
16161 Brookpark Road, Cleveland, Ohio

South Sea Island
14916 Puritas Avenue, Cleveland, Ohio

An advertisement for the Aloha-Kai, which offered Clevelanders the newest and most unique Polynesian Restaurant and Tiki Lounge. *Courtesy of Scott Schell.*

4

TOLEDO

Toledo has always been a mecca for live entertainment. This may have been due to the number of club owners and the mob bosses that were centered in the city, but the city has also always been known for its extravagant nightclubs and talented musicians. Many of these clubs are long gone, but places like the Cocoanut Grove in the 1930s, La Conga Room and the Latin Club in the 1940s were showcases for some of the country's top entertainment. Even Tony Packo's Nite Club packed in club goers in the 1950s, before becoming famous for its hot dogs.

It wasn't until 1960, when mob figure and former nightclub owner Irving "Slick" Shapiro opened the Aku-Aku in the Town House Motel, that Toledo became a major hub for gangsters to mingle and catch top entertainers like Duke Ellington and Count Basie.

While downtown residents knew the culinary scene included a diverse collection of local delights, the city really didn't have many Hawaiian-themed restaurants. I've included as many as I could locate in this chapter but not much is known about them. Even the Aku-Aku left much to be desired in the way of tropical décor, but it was the club's drinks and the entertainment that kept people coming back.

AKU-AKU POLYNESIAN ROOM AT THE TOWN HOUSE MOTEL

1111 West Bancroft Street, Toledo, Ohio

The Aku-Aku Polynesian Room used photographs of Oceanic art pieces on their menus. *Author's collection.*

The Aku-Aku Polynesian Room at the Town House Motel was one of the last great Polynesian supper clubs in Ohio. The hotel complex was originally supposed to be named the Stardust, but it was quickly changed due to another Stardust hotel being located in Las Vegas. The club was owned by Irving "Slick" Shapiro, a bookmaker with several arrests under his belt by the time the Aku-Aku officially opened on December 13, 1960. He was a gracious host with a sense of humor and often greeted people as they walked in the door. For over a decade, the place was famous for hosting some of the biggest names in the entertainment industry; Duke Ellington, Count Basie, Tony Bennett and the Glenn Miller Orchestra all played there. The Aku-Aku even had its own Polynesian review every night by Moana and her Islanders. It was definitely the hip place to be in the 1960s.

Toledo was considered a safe haven for mobsters, and they often attended the Aku-Aku and were seated behind a curtained-off section of the dining room so as not to draw attention to themselves as they watched the show. From 1971 to 1972, the place was under new management and featured more local bands. In 1972, the Town House Motel closed after going into foreclosure, and the site was sold at a sheriff's auction to recover debt owed to the bank. It eventually reopened as the University Inn, a truck stop hotel in 1973, before closing its doors for good in 1984. The building sat empty for five years before being demolished in 1989. A Rally's drive-thru now occupies the site. Chester Devenow, a retired chairman of the former Sheller-Globe Corporation, said Toledo will never see a place like the Aku-Aku club again. "It was a gathering place for the top and bottom of society—the elite to the lowest characters that Toledo had to offer. It was the last important gathering place for the last generation of Toledo."

While the Aku-Aku has an impressive history and some stunning use of Tiki iconography, the room itself was streamlined and modern. This was quite the opposite of the immersive faux paradise more commonly known in the 1960s. According to *Book of Tiki* author Sven Kirsten, "The Aku-Aku is a great example of mid-century modern restaurants that were not expressively Polynesian in décor but lived their exotic-ness through their cocktails."

OTHER TOLEDO TIKI RESTAURANTS

Aloha Supper Club
2947 Tremainsville Road, Toledo, Ohio

Club Aloha
5035 Alexis Road, Toledo, Ohio

The Islander and Islander II
1518 and 1540 Sylvania Avenue, Toledo, Ohio

Art's Safari Club
3835 North Detroit Street, Toledo, Ohio

Tot's Tropics or Tot's Coral Room
Lorraine Hotel, Jefferson at Twelfth, Toledo Ohio

Bamboo Club
Huron Street at LaGrange, Toledo, Ohio

The Taboo Lounge
Hotel Willard, Adams and St. Clair Streets,
Toledo, Ohio

A rare ashtray from the Taboo Lounge in Toledo, Ohio. *Author's collection.*

5

DAYTON

Dayton has solid roots in Tiki history. The city was once home to George Rudin's Tropics, which predated the Kahiki by seven years and was the first large-scale Polynesian-themed restaurant in the state—it was extremely successful. In 1960, famed Tiki carver Barney West made four large Tiki carvings for the Tropics and had them shipped to Dayton. West carved Tikis for Trader Vic's, the Tropics and hundreds of other restaurants, shopping centers and resorts that were in need of Polynesian décor. Dayton supper club Johnny K's Reef also played a role in promoting the island atmosphere.

In February 1961, the Cox Municipal Airport, now the Dayton International Airport, constructed a terminal building at a cost of $5 million. A Polynesian restaurant and an array of offices and shops were all planned to be included in the new terminal. The Polynesian restaurant was to be operated by Dobb's House Inc., which already owned a number of successful Hawaiian-themed restaurants in Memphis and Atlanta known as the Dobb's House Luau.

In a letter to his stockholders J.K. Dobbs wrote:

> *There is one thing we are excited about and that is our new Polynesian restaurants. We are now putting one in Dallas and one in Miami and will probably put one in Dayton. (Incidentally, we have just been awarded a new 15-year lease there). They are going to build a new airport, and we intend to have a Polynesian dining room as well as the regular coffee shop. It seems to us that the formal dining rooms are things of the past. Our Polynesian*

NOW APPEARING

BOBBY MONAHAN

That genuinely funny man, better known as—

MR. FIVE BY FIVE

SUPERIOR CUISINE FOR DISCRIMINATING TASTE ... SET IN THE DELIGHTFUL ATMOSPHERE OF THE WEST INDIES

Luncheon ... A delightful (and reasonable) respite from shopping or business.

217 N. Main St. — BA 4-8341

Above: An advertisement for the Caribbean, nautical-themed bar, Johnny K's Reef, in Dayton, Ohio. *Author's collection*.

Left: A menu from the Dobb's House Luau restaurant that never quite made it to Dayton International Airport. *Author's collection*.

Early advertising for Georgie Rudin's Tropics in Dayton, Ohio. *Courtesy of Natalie Rudin-Cohn.*

restaurants will be similar to Trader Vic's, Don the Beachcomber, and so forth. We have everybody in the organization, that is, all the cooks, chefs, and so forth, working on Polynesian food, and we just know we are going to give the people the finest Polynesian food in the world.

Prior to opening, the Polynesian theme was abandoned by city commissioners, who opted to go with an "Early American" theme. The Dobb's House restaurant and coffee shop operated for fifteen years, but it is unfortunate that the proposed little Polynesia at the Dobbs Airport Lounge never materialized.

GEORGE RUDIN'S TROPICS

1721 North Main Street, Dayton, Ohio

George Rudin (or "Georgie," as his friends called him) was born on February 24, 1916, in Middletown, Ohio. His father immigrated to the United States from Russia and settled in Middletown to work for the American Rolling Mill Company (ARMCO), a large steel manufacturer. During World War

75

II, George found work at his cousin's tire shop in Detroit. Because money was tight, he decided to live at the downtown YMCA, which just happened to be located across the street from the Hotel Wolverine. The hotel was prestigious, and it had an adjoining nightclub called the Tropics. At the time, the Tropics was Michigan's most unusual nightspot and cocktail lounge. The interior décor created the mood of the South Seas, complete with a waterfall tumbling down behind the bar, bamboo, palm trees and other tropical touches. Orchestras provided exotica music and lured couples out onto a dance floor that was covered in multicolored lights. Upon entering a place like the Tropics in the middle of an industrialized city like Detroit, one can only imagine what George was thinking. It undoubtedly left a lasting impression.

In 1944, George moved back to Dayton and opened a drive-in fruit stand at 1721 North Main Street; his grandfather previously owned a grocery store on Wayne Avenue. George bought all of his fruits and vegetables from Roy Pinsky and Company in Dayton. Pinsky's was a family-owned wholesale business that supplied fresh fruits and vegetables to local restaurants, supermarkets, schools and hospitals. Its warehouse was located on the corner of Patterson Boulevard and St. Clair Street. In 1946, the nation was still weary from the war and suddenly found itself in a meat shortage. George made a deal with the Kahn's Meat Company of Cincinnati to sell its meat exclusively. This was a smart move on George's part, as his Main Street location became the main source for meat in the entire state of Ohio. The store was selling thirty to forty thousand pounds of meat per day and supplying the local restaurants as well. "There was a great demand for meat," George exclaimed. "We would admit one hundred people per hour and that went on all day. We sold thirty sides of beef per day and one thousand pounds of bacon a day." They also purchased prized meats from the Pfaelzer Brothers in Chicago to use for steaks. When the meat shortage came to an end, George thought about what he could to do next.

As much as he enjoyed the financial gain of the grocery store at the time, George had bigger ambitions and was inspired by the restaurant and nightclub he saw in Detroit. In 1947, George obtained a liquor license and never looked back. The grocery store turned into a cocktail lounge and deli, and George purchased two barbecue spits to rotate and cook meat. These cookers were strategically placed in the window so that people could see the meat cooking. The deli was so popular that a large patio had to be built outside to accommodate more customers. Originally, the deli only had

Left: The front cover of a menu from the Tropics at the Hotel Wolverine in Detroit, Michigan. *Author's collection*.

Below: A postcard showing the interior of the Tropics nightclub inside the Hotel Wolverine. *Courtesy of Scott Schell*.

George Rudin posing with the Kahn's meatpackers in Cincinnati, Ohio. *Courtesy of Natalie Rudin-Cohn.*

seats for 77 people, which gradually expanded to 145. With an increase in business, another expansion became necessary; George made more room by using the alley behind his building for more seating. The outside patio was eventually closed in, and a Hawaiian motif soon began to take shape. George named the place the Tropics, and his idea for a grand Polynesian supper club began to form.

In 1952, George hired Don Rosset and his wife, Ruth, to help with a $35,000 expansion project. Don and his wife ran a contracting and interior decorating business and were only eager to help. The enclosed patio was replaced by a large dining room. Folding doors were built in to divide the dining room and cocktail lounge in half. After 9:00 p.m. the doors would be closed, and the southern half of the club would be turned into a giant cocktail lounge. A revolving stage was constructed to give the room continuous entertainment. Bennie Berlin, George's brother-in-law, was brought in to do all the bamboo work. Berlin also managed the kitchen in the daytime and oversaw the receiving department. Oh, and according to Natalie Rudin-Cohn, he grew tomatoes up on the roof.

An interior view of George Rudin's supermarket and delicatessen, when it was still just the beginning of an idea. *Courtesy of Natalie Rudin-Cohn.*

An early shot of the exterior of George Rudin's Tropics Supper Club. *Courtesy of Natalie Rudin-Cohn.*

A beautiful shot of a young George Rudin in front one of the large murals inside the restaurant. *Photo by Lee Ayres, courtesy of Natalie Rudin-Cohn.*

In April 1953, work was nearing completion on another expansion when a devastating fire destroyed the building. George estimated that he lost around $95,000 in the fire and that most of the restaurant's equipment and furnishings were lost. Undaunted by the devastation, George started making plans to rebuild his dream Polynesian supper club.

The neon Tropics sign welcomed all of the late-night party goers. Photo by Keller Studio. *Courtesy of Natalie Rudin-Cohn.*

On November 18, 1954, the Tropics officially reopened. For the grand opening, they hired Momikai and her Tropical Islanders as the main attraction. Momikai had a long history in the Hawaiian-themed entertainment industry; she played the famous Hawaiian Room at the Lexington Hotel in New York for nine years and was also a member of the Lani McIntire group. Before coming to the Tropics, she sang at the Waikiki Club in Chicago. Momikai also appeared on the Don Williams Show on WHIO-TV on channel seven every day from 4:00 to 5:00 p.m. The famous Latin American singer Jose Madrigal strolled among the patrons and sang requests on opening night.

The Tropics featured some of the biggest names in the entertainment industry. In 1953, Goodie (Goodwin) Sable left the RKO theater chain and accepted the position of maître d' at George Rudin's Tropics Supper Club. It was a natural position for Goodie, who was good looking, lovable and always well-mannered. Goodie was a walking encyclopedia of show business, which he got caught up in while working for Johnny Harris in Pennsylvania. At the time, Johnny Harris was known as "Mr. Show Business of Pittsburgh." Harris was the original Ice Capades owner, and Goodie managed the roller-skating portion of the business. When Goodie moved to Dayton in 1934, he accepted the position of assistant manager at the Strand Theatre. Later, he also managed the State, Colonial and Keith Theatres. He would eventually manage all three RKO theatres in Dayton from 1947 to 1953. Throughout the years, Goodie established lasting friendships with many of the stars from the music industry and the stage and screen. Some of the famous celebrities he met included Cab Calloway, Louis Armstrong, Jackie Gleason, Gene Krupa, Perry Como and many more. Sometimes, Goodie even invited celebrities to his home; he really took a personal interest in the performers he liked. He had an infectious personality and would even visit the performers backstage before and after each show to provide his support. After six memorable years at the Tropics, Goodie accepted positions at the Racquet Club, the Shrimp Boat and finally to the King Cole restaurant.

Above: The Tropics Supper Club's Polynesian Room in Dayton, Ohio. *Courtesy of Natalie Rudin-Cohn.*

Opposite, top: The Tropics Supper Club's Waikiki Room in Dayton, Ohio. *Courtesy of Natalie Rudin-Cohn.*

Opposite, bottom: The Tropics Supper Club's Outrigger Bar in Dayton, Ohio. *Courtesy of Natalie Rudin-Cohn.*

His wife, Sarah, said, "Pleasing people is what he loves." Goodie replied, "It's my therapy—it keeps me going." The Tropics became one of the biggest and busiest supper clubs in Ohio.

In 1960, Barney West completed and shipped four large Tikis to the Tropics. Each measured about six feet tall and weighed close to six hundred pounds—they were carved out of solid sycamore logs. George loved to remodel and was always making trips to Hawaii and the Philippines to buy surfboards, outrigger canoes, Tiki gods and other tropical artifacts. At its peak, the restaurant boasted five different rooms: the Waikiki Room, the Polynesian Room, the Bamboo Lounge, the Outrigger Bar and the Surfboard Lounge.

The Tropics Supper Club's Surfboard Lounge in Dayton, Ohio. *Courtesy of Natalie Rudin-Cohn.*

During the discotheque go-go craze of the 1960s, Rudin hired attractive young women to be trained as dancers. There was go-go dancing on the main stage and at the bar. After a couple of years, George abandoned the go-go idea, stating, "Go-go suddenly became very risqué, and we didn't want that kind of thing here."

In August 1987, the restaurant closed after more than forty years in business. George held onto the property for another eight years before eventually selling it. In 1988, George held an auction and sale to get rid of many of the items that were inside the club. In 1994, the property was sold to the Revco Drug Store chain, and the building was razed.

The following is an interview with Natalie Rudin-Cohn, the daughter of George Rudin.

> *JEFF CHENAULT. What kind of person was your dad?*
> *NATALIE RUDIN-COHN. He was an outgoing guy, but he never told risqué jokes. He listened to people. He never told stories about anything that*

Go-go girls inside the Outrigger Room and Showbar at the Tropics Supper Club. *Courtesy of Natalie Rudin-Cohn.*

went on in the restaurant. Whatever happened at the Tropics stayed at the Tropics. He had a lot of friends. They could confide in him and talk with him. He liked to entertain. He would have some of the entertainers come to our house and cook. My dad had a nice house on Heather Drive in North Dayton. The area was just being developed, and we were one of the first to move there.

JEFF. Describe a typical day for your dad.

NATALIE. He would leave home around 4:00 p.m., and worked until 2:00 a.m. Then at 5:00 a.m., he would pick up the fresh fruit and vegetables from Pinsky's to use later that day. He loved his work, and it showed.

JEFF. Did you ever work at the restaurant?

NATALIE. Only on New Year's Eve, occasionally as a hostess. My mother always went to the airport to get the lobster. My dad had a contract with a company in Maine. When my kids were little, they would go with their grandmother to pick up the lobsters and tell me about the hissing sound they made.

A well-dressed Georgie Rudin inside the Bamboo Lounge. *Courtesy of Natalie Rudin-Cohn.*

JEFF. Who were some of the people that worked at the restaurant?

NATALIE. Goodie Sable. He was a maître d'. Before that, he was the manager for the three RKO theaters in town. His wife's name was Sarah. They never had any children. They used to come to the house. He was kind of portly and very smooth. Everybody loved him.

JEFF. Who ran the kitchen?

NATALIE. My dad ran the kitchen. When he first opened the restaurant, he had two barbecue spits in the window, just like they had at the Old Hickory restaurant on Brown Street. You could actually see it cooking. When they renovated, it all went away. It lasted a good ten years though.

JEFF. Did he like to cook?

NATALIE. No, but he hired people to do that and made up some of the recipes. He created the chicken almondine and the chicken velvet. They never called it Chinese, it was always Polynesian. Oh, and he had a pupu platter—I wish I had a picture of that. It had rumaki and those little baby ribs and the meat on the stick with the little fire

Left: The Tropics Supper Club's drink menu. *Courtesy of Natalie Rudin-Cohn.*

Right: A close-up of the Tropics' Pagan's Brew Tiki Bowl, which was served nightly at the Tropics Supper Club. *Courtesy of Natalie Rudin-Cohn.*

underneath. I could just have dinner on that pupu platter and not eat another thing. My dad also served three complimentary condiments: cottage cheese with chives, real dill pickles out of a barrel and one other thing. Then, he'd charge three dollars for dinner, and people would still complain. Can you imagine?

JEFF. I bet the bar was always busy.

NATALIE. It was a real hangout. At 5:00, all these executives would come from their businesses. It would be five people deep at the bar. You couldn't get a seat. It was packed. And they drank hard liquor. I don't drink at all. I could never tolerate it.

JEFF. Was your dad aware of the competition?

NATALIE. I didn't know there were so many of them. I never heard of all these places. I wonder if my dad ever went to any of them. I never heard him mention it. Not too long ago, a couple I knew, who were in the antiques business, had the nerve to call their new restaurant the Tropics. It was in Lincoln Park. I called the state to see if dad had a copyright on the name, but he didn't. I was insulted, but their restaurant just fell flat. I

The Vicious Virgin mug was a favorite at the Tropics Supper Club, but today, the mugs are very difficult to find. *Courtesy of Natalie Rudin-Cohn.*

don't think it was open more than six months. I was kind of embarrassed that they would do such a thing and do such a bad job at it.

JEFF. Any other fond memories you'd like to share?

NATALIE. They were all fond memories. Just seeing people there that I knew all the time and partying. New Year's Eve was always a party. There were a lot of fond memories because of all the celebrities that I got to meet. I met Liza Minnelli, Jackie Gleason and so many others. I was infatuated by Hollywood when I was younger and the Tropics always brought them in.

KON-TIKI THEATRE

4100 Salem Avenue, Dayton, Ohio

The Kon-Tiki Theatre was a Polynesian-themed cinema located in Trotwood, Ohio, a suburb of Dayton. The theater officially opened in August 1968, and it was modeled after the Grauman's Chinese Theatre in Hollywood. The theater was originally owned and operated by Sam Levin, the owner of the Levin Theatre Company. Sam was a businessman who owned multiple businesses, theaters and drive-ins around the Cincinnati area. The Kon-Tiki Theatre was loaded with a mixture of South Pacific and Asian décor. There were illuminated Tiki masks on the theater's façade, and a mixture of volcanic rock and abalone shells were built into its walls. Even the restrooms had sinks made from giant clamshells! The theater was operated by the Levin family until May 13, 1987. The first movie shown in the theatre was *The Odd Couple*, which stars Jack Lemmon and Walter Matthau. The theater had one screen when it opened, but a second auditorium was later added and the original screen was divided, making it a triplex. At that point, the theater was renamed Kon-Tiki Cinemas 1-2-3. In 1987, the building was leased to USA Cinemas, which renamed the theater Salem Avenue Cinemas. USA Cinemas was later acquired by the Loew's chain, and the name changed again to Loews Salem Ave. Over time, extensive damage was done to the building by vandals breaking in and some busted water pipes that left a nasty mold problem. The theater closed in February 1999, and the Levin brothers, who still owned the building, donated the Kon-Tiki and its land to the City of Trotwood. The building was razed in January 2005 to allow for redevelopment of the space.

BLUE HAWAII RESTAURANT

Dayton, Ohio

The Blue Hawaii Restaurant was owned by the House of Linn and Lu from Formosa. They owned about twelve restaurants, each run separately by different family members. Frank Linn, who was already operating a restaurant in Indianapolis, was persuaded to open a Polynesian restaurant in Dayton by Wright-Patterson Air Force Base employees, who praised the virtues of the area. The place was authentic in décor and had seating for 120 people.

SAFARI CLUB

205 Ludlow, Dayton, Ohio

The "swinging" Safari Club in Dayton was, by all accounts, a go-go bar—a place to swing with the swingers. Music was provided by Souls Inc and other various musical and comedy acts. The club's burlesque dancers included Candy, Pinky and their very own Safari Club dancers. The club advertised as having a tropical atmosphere, but if this just meant that there was a bamboo pole on the main stage, no one would be surprised.

6

MISCELLANEOUS TIKI

Major cities weren't the only places you could have a Polynesian dinner or a tropical cocktail. Some of the most unique places in Ohio existed outside city limits. These places were usually owned by people who not only had a passion for tropical décor but also had a keen business sense. It was intriguing to find such an abundance of places like bowling alleys and McDonald's locations all with a Hawaiian motif. Some of these places were obscure and little information is known about them. I have listed these places to be as comprehensive as possible and with the hope of uncovering more information in the future. Sometimes, a newspaper advertisement or a tattered matchbook cover was the only proof of a restaurant's existence. In this chapter, you will also read about places that never made it past the planning stages.

BALI HAI (NOW KNOWN AS THE HUNAN BALI HAI)

25649 Euclid Avenue, Euclid, Ohio

The Bali Hai was a Chinese-Polynesian restaurant that also had a complete American menu as well. The décor inside the restaurant wasn't very tropical; it had more of an Asian atmosphere, with Chinese lanterns and the like. What the restaurant did have in the way of Polynesian décor was an amazing palm tree neon sign out front with an equally gorgeous menu that was also covered in palm trees. The Bali Hai served exotic tropical drinks including the Mai Tai, Planter's Punch, the Zombie and their very own drink called the Bali Hai Tiki Swizzle. Customers could only order one Swizzle per person, so it must have packed quite a punch. The drink menu even had a Tiki on it!

An inside look at a matchbook from the Bol-A-Kai located in Bedford, Ohio. *Courtesy of Scott Schell.*

A dinner menu from McGarvey's Beachcomber in Grand River, Ohio. *Courtesy of Scott Schell.*

BOL-A-KAI

400 Northfield Road, Bedford, Ohio

The Bol-A-Kai was a unique Polynesian-themed restaurant, lounge and bowling alley in the Cleveland suburbs of Bedford, Ohio. The Bol-A-Kai was owned by George Goudreau, and it served up authentic Polynesian delicacies and cocktails in the thrilling atmosphere of the islands. The only picture I could find was on a matchbook, which shows the large A-frame sign that was located just outside the restaurant.

McGARVEY'S BEACHCOMBER

108 Henry Street, Grand River, Ohio

McGarvey's Beachcomber was a landmark restaurant owned by Charles "Charlie" McGarvey. It was located thirty miles east of Cleveland near Painesville. The McGarveys also owned two other nautical restaurants called McGarvey's Party House in Lorain and McGarvey's Nautical Restaurant in Vermillion. The McGarvey family sold the restaurant to Charles Solomon, who would run the restaurant with his brother, Eddie Solomon. The Solomon family ran the restaurant under the McGarvey name for the next forty-five years. The menu exclaimed, "We are happy you chose to sail with us on a dining adventure." It was the largest seafood chain in Ohio at the time. The restaurant also had a nice-looking Beachcomber sign out front that was flanked by two carved Tikis.

DIAMOND HEAD

33 North Paint Street, Chillicothe, Ohio

The Diamond Head restaurant was owned by Peter Lin. His Polynesian-style restaurant opened in 1978. It was located inside the former dining room of the Warner building in downtown Chillicothe. It served Chinese and American foods as well as Polynesian drinks and cocktails. The interior was decorated in a Hawaiian–Polynesian style, and the restaurant's menu had a strange-looking Tiki on it. Peter Lin operated many restaurants, including the China Garden in Portsmouth. This was his second restaurant in Ohio.

MILANO'S TIKI AND THE MILANO CLUB

415 West Market Street, Lima, Ohio

Milano's is a Lima institution. Since the 1960s, the restaurant was famous for its Old-World Italian food. Sometime during the 1960s, the restaurant operated a Tiki bar inside this establishment. A matchbook is the only surviving proof of its existence. The restaurant is family owned and operated by Frank Guagenti. The location on Market Street in downtown Lima was the original location until a fire destroyed the building in 1996. The restaurant was rebuilt in another existing restaurant called Tudor's, which the family also owned. Today, the family legacy lives on, and the Guagentis continue to serve some of the best Italian food in Ohio. Their restaurant's new location is at 2383 Elida Road in Lima.

CLUB ZOMBIE

612 West Perkins Avenue, Sandusky, Ohio

The Club Zombie was a popular hub in the 1940s. It may have been named after the successful Club Zombie located inside the Hawley House in Cleveland. Unfortunately, this location closed in 1947, and it was replaced by the Top Hat.

FIJI ISLAND RESTAURANT

718 Illinois, Maumee, Ohio

The Fiji Island Restaurant was another attempt at serving exotic drinks and Chinese, Polynesian and American foods inside a Hawaiian atmosphere. The décor was done very well, and the restaurant had a ton of bamboo lining its walls and ceiling. The restaurant even had plants and other décor hanging from its ceiling. One wall had a huge dragon painting on it, and the tables all had Tiki lamps on them. Hula girls and Tikis graced the Fiji Island Restaurant's menus and matchbook covers. This Polynesian paradise in Maumee, Ohio, spared no expense in the décor department.

LEHMANN'S LODGE

Route 18, Fostoria, Ohio

Lehmann's Lodge opened in 1963 at a cost of over $100,000. The complex consisted of a motel, a 150-seat restaurant, a lounge, a 250-seat banquet room, an indoor swimming pool, a billiards room and an indoor 9-hole mini golf. The lodge's restaurant was described as having a Polynesian setting with Chinese food. It was also said to have had bamboo on its ceiling, which was supported by carved Tiki posts.

TIKI McDONALD'S

4571 Kent Road, Stow, Ohio

Yes, there truly was a Tiki McDonald's. It was owned by Richard Heidman and opened in 1984. Heidman owned several McDonald's locations in and around the Akron area. All of them were themed and very popular. I visited this particular location in the late 1990s when my friend and musician Andy Izold, who lived in Cuyahoga Falls, suggested we check it out. Sure enough, the space was full of Hawaiian décor, Tiki masks and a large carved Tiki, which was there to greet you as you ate your Big Mac and French fries. One wall in the dining area was made of glass; on the other side of the wall, there was a narrow room made to look like a jungle with parrots in it. Every fifteen minutes or so, the lights would flicker, an audio recording of thunder would play and

Tiki Oasis founder Otto von Stroheim visiting the Tiki McDonalds in Stow, Ohio. *Courtesy of Otto von Stroheim.*

water would run down the glass to look like rain. The owners were obviously lovers of tropical décor. The feeling was strange and surreal.

Tiki veteran Otto Von Stroheim, who also visited this location in the late 1990s, had this to say:

> *The entire McDonald's was Tiki style, including tapa patterns etched into glass dividers on booth walls, the color of the seating, the plants, some of the signage and lots of masks, Tikis and war clubs attached to the walls. Some of the décor was from Oceanic Arts, but I believe the Tikis were carved locally.*

Ohio lounge enthusiast and Tikiphile Michael Toth also remembers the restaurant well:

> *While it was nothing special from the outside, an enclosed "rain forest" was built around the perimeter, creating an exotic locale when looking out.*

Live birds, in cages and flying free, shared the enclosure with tropical plants. Inside the enclosure, the temperature and humidity of an actual rainforest was maintained. The birds and plants were identified on informative wooden panels beside the windows. The Kahiki in Columbus had a similar thing in one of its sections, which could be where they got the idea. Every twenty minutes, there were lightning effects and thunder and rain sounds as the enclosure was sprayed with water. I think there were also tribal drums in between the "rainstorms." Glass panels that divided the booths had primitive mask designs etched into them, and Polynesian statues peered out over the burger devourers. It was inexplicably bizarre.

It's not certain when this McDonald's went out of business, or when and if it changed ownership, but the building was torn down and is now an empty lot. With any luck, the owners found another restaurant to decorate and enjoy. Their enthusiasm and love for Hawaiian culture brought a unique look to the interior of this fast food restaurant.

BALI HAI

4508 Lincoln Way East, Massillon, Ohio 44646

The Bali Hai in Massillon was Northeast Ohio's premier Polynesian lounge and restaurant. It was opened in 1960 by Emil Chapanar. The location was midway between Pittsburgh and Chicago on the historic Lincoln Highway. The Bali Hai was a popular stop for hungry travelers of that era who were traveling between New York City and San Francisco. It was one of the first restaurants in Stark County to feature Chinese food. The famous Moonlight Ballroom and the Casablanca Nightclub were both located within five miles of the Bali Hai, so there are plenty of locals with stories of celebrity sightings. The Bali Hai's name was inspired by the song of the same name in the musical *South Pacific*. When Emil's wife, Helen, saw the film in 1959, she instantly fell in love with Hawaiian culture. After a fire in 1966, the Bali Hai underwent extensive remodeling for the better. The Bali Hai had an amazing Tiki neon sign out front that complemented the A-frame building and Polynesian architecture. The restaurant also had gas-lit Tiki torches and a giant Moai placed out front to welcome traveling guests.

THE DESHLER HILTON
Columbus, Ohio

Above: The Kahiki Supper Club circa 1965 was one of the most beautiful Polynesian restaurants in the world. *Author's collection.*

Left: The Top of the Isle was a unique Polynesian restaurant with a downtown view from the twelfth floor of the Deshler-Hilton Hotel. *Author's collection.*

Above: Master chef and Kahiki veteran Soeng Thong serving up a roast suckling pig for Sunday brunch at the Tropical Bistro. *Author's collection*.

Right: Grass Skirt Tiki Bar owner Carmen Owens in her element. *Courtesy of Mitch Geiser*.

Top: This mysterious Tiki was purchased from an antique store in South Carolina and resided at the Grass Skirt Tiki Bar in Columbus, Ohio. *Author's collection*.

Bottom: This well-preserved and maintained Kahiki artifact named George could be found on display at the Grass Skirt Tiki Bar in Columbus, Ohio. *Author's collection*.

This original Grass Skirt
Tiki Bar poster, made by
artist Clinton Reno, captures
the true spirit of Ohio Tiki.
Courtesy of Clinton Reno.

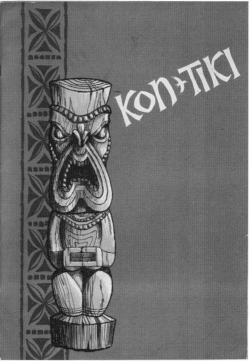

Stephan Crane's Kon-Tiki is a
delightful diversion, especially
when it is ordered with a Mai Tai.
Author's collection.

Top: You know it's a good day when drinks like Steve's Rum Barrel, the Coffee Grog, the Tiger's Milk and the Zombie are all on the same page. *Courtesy of Scott Schell.*

Bottom: The Bamboo Room at the Hotel Olmsted in Cleveland, Ohio, lived up to its name by having wall-to-wall bamboo paneling. *Courtesy of Scott Schell.*

Above: Boasting five separate rooms filled with tropical decor, the Tropics was the first large-scale Polynesian supper club in Ohio. It was also the longest-lasting. *Courtesy of Scott Schell*.

Right: Natalie Rudin-Cohn (daughter of George Rudin) proudly holds up one of her father's dinner menus. *Author's collection*.

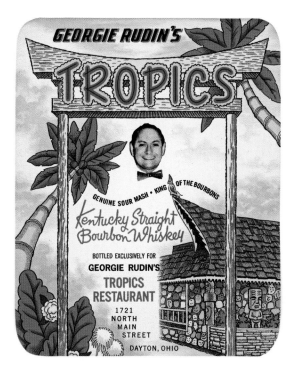

Left: Label art for Kentucky Straight Bourbon Whiskey, which was exclusively bottled for George Rudin's Tropics restaurant. *Courtesy of Natalie Rudin-Cohn.*

Below: This collector's showcase, or drinker's checklist, of the drinks and vessels contained in The Tropics drink menu is highly desirable. *Courtesy of Natalie Rudin-Cohn.*

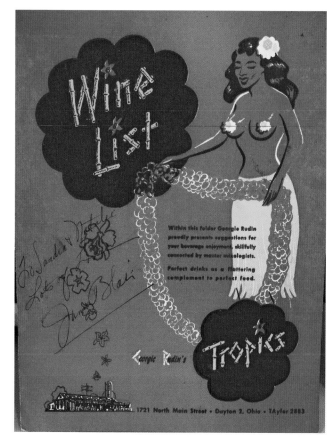

Right: George Rudin also catered to vino connoisseurs by offering an extensive collection of vintage wine. *Courtesy of Natalie Rudin-Cohn*.

Below: Rare homemade ceramics from an unknown artist with gold Tropics logos. *Courtesy of Natalie Rudin-Cohn*.

The Diamond Head's drink menu separates drinks that are romantic, passionate and wild. *Courtesy of Scott Schell.*

A bountiful harvest awaits you in the Hawaiian Punch Village at Sea World in Aurora, Ohio. *Courtesy of Scott Schell.*

Above: This is the original photo that was used for the cover of the Beachcomber Trio album *Live at the Kahiki*. It was released on Dionysus Records in 2010. *Author's collection.*

Left; A Bon Voyage Kahiki postcard with original artwork by Dirty Donny. *Author's collection.*

Right: The famous bartender known only as "Skip" having way too much fun at the Kahiki. *Courtesy of Linda Sapp-Long.*

Below: Original painting *Kahalu'u Sunset* by famed Hawaiian artist Herb Kane. The models in the photo are Francis Llacuna, his wife, Gloria, and their daughter, Fran. *Courtesy of Francis Llacuna.*

Above: John Holt, who was also known as Tiki Skip, on top of the largest Kahiki souvenir ever! *Photo by Eric Albrecht, courtesy of* Columbus Dispatch.

Left: A Smoking Rum Punch for Two from the Grass Skirt Tiki Bar in Columbus, Ohio. *Courtesy of Brock Ailes*.

Top: The Blue Hawaiian Cocktail from the Grass Skirt Tiki Bar in Columbus, Ohio. *Courtesy of Brock Ailes.*

Bottom: The February 1962 issue of *American Restaurant* featured Marsh Padilla and the Beachcomber Trio playing inside the Kahiki Supper Club on the front cover. *Author's collection.*

Left: Casablanca Drink Menu—an early drink menu from Tully Foster's Casablanca Supper Club, a famous watering hole near Canton in the 1940s. *Author's collection*.

Below: Hawaiian Luau Miami University—a Hawaiian luau and entertainment menu from the fourth-annual Civil Air Patrol National Aviation and Education Workshop. The event was held at Miami University in Oxford, Ohio, in 1952. *Courtesy of Scott Schell*.

Kahiki glass art made by Velvet Glass in Tucson, Arizona. The original piece is owned by Caroline Rowe. *Courtesy of Maggie Rickard and Mark Bloom.*

Kahiki Moai enjoying another day of guarding the entrance to the Kahiki. *Courtesy of Linda Sapp-Long.*

Above: A Kahiki Party with Dave Thomas, the founder of Wendy's Hamburgers, joining in on the fun. *Author's collection*.

Left: This beautiful Tiki from the Kahiki now resides in the collection of Jim and Elise Robinson. *Author's collection*.

A matchbook from the Bali Hai Restaurant in Massillon, Ohio. *Courtesy of Scott Schell.*

Ohio musician and Tikiphile Pablus has fond memories of the Bali Hai.

My Uncle Bill (Simmons), nicknamed "Sarge," was the bartender at the Bali Hai for years. Many of the Rat Pack and other mob-connected folks would come in with their cronies from Youngstown and quaff drinks at a premier Tiki bar without having to go into Cleveland, which was a risky proposition in those days. After a few years, my uncle opened up his own Polynesian speakeasy in a back alley of downtown Massillon, where the Hideaway bar stands today. It was very short-lived but was loaded with vintage Witco and other Polynesian décor. Legend has it that Frank Sinatra and Joey Bishop visited a few times as well.

The Bali Hai was remodeled in 1971, but the restaurant sadly closed its doors for good in 1984.

THE CASTAWAY BAR

Route 534, Geneva on the Lake, Ohio

Geneva on the Lake was a hugely popular tourist destination and was commonly known as Ohio's first summer resort. The central attraction to the area was the "Strip" on State Route 53. The Strip was lined with a

GENEVA-ON-THE-LAKE, OHIO

Left: A napkin from the Castaway Restaurant in Geneva-On-The-Lake, Ohio. *Courtesy of Scott Schell.*

Below: A Castaway Restaurant advertisement. The Castaway was the only Polynesian restaurant where you had to walk through a Tiki's mouth to enter the building. *Courtesy of Scott Schell.*

multitude of parks, bars, restaurants and arcades. Owned by Jimmy Brown, the Castaway Bar was a tropical-themed restaurant that boasted a huge Tiki with gas-lit, flaming eyes at the entranceway. To enter the building, customers had to walk through the giant concrete Tiki's mouth. Carved Tiki poles circled the outside of the building. During the 1960s, dancers would pull out a portable shower from behind the bar and perform the "Shower Au-Go Go" dance routine. Boy, times have changed. Country star Conway Twitty performed here and released an album of the recordings. Sadly, the restaurant succumbed to the times and faded into obscurity.

BAMBOO GARDENS

5871 Mayfield Heights, Ohio

The Bamboo Gardens was an Oriental–Polynesian restaurant owned by Jimmie and Joan Chin. Chef Jew Hong Chin, Joan's brother-in-law, and Buddy Wu supervised the restaurant's food preparation. In 1988, the restaurant won the fried chicken category in the National Chicken Out Festival. The late Jimmie Chin developed the recipe. I offer you the award-winning recipe for the Bamboo Gardens' Tiki Chicken below, along with the accompanying Tiki sauce. The restaurant's property is now the location of a Golden Dragon Chinese restaurant.

Bamboo Gardens' Tiki Chicken

¾ cup all-purpose flour
I tablespoon baking powder
I tablespoon cornstarch
4 eggs, lightly beaten
I teaspoon water
I tablespoon corn oil
Corn oil for deep frying
8 large chicken breast halves, skinned and boned
Salt and white pepper
Fried rice or white rice
Tiki Sauce (recipe follows)
3 green onions, chopped
8 spears fresh pineapple with green top attached

In a small bowl, combine flour, baking powder and cornstarch. Add eggs and water and whisk until smooth. Whisk in I tablespoon corn oil. Heat corn oil to 375 degrees. Sprinkle chicken with salt and pepper. Dip into batter, drain off excess and deep fry until a light golden brown. Drain on paper towels.

Let oil cool to 355 degrees. Return chicken to oil, and cook for about 4 to 6 minutes, until cooked through. Hold it under the oil during cooking. Drain on towels, then cut into strips ¾ to I inch wide. Place strips on top of rice. Top with Tiki Sauce and sprinkle with chopped green onions. Garnish each plate with a fresh pineapple spear. Makes 8 servings.

Tiki Sauce

1 tablespoon corn oil
1 clove garlic, mashed
2 cups water
1 cup ketchup
2 tablespoons vinegar (apple cider or white wine)
3 tablespoons sugar
½ lemon
2 tablespoons cornstarch
2 tablespoons water

In a small saucepan, heat oil and sauté garlic until golden but not brown. Stir in water, ketchup, vinegar and sugar. Cut the lemon half in half again. Squeeze in the juice, then add the two quarters. Bring to a boil over high heat, stirring, then boil gently for about 3 minutes. Pour through a strainer and return to saucepan. Combine cornstarch and water; stir mixture into sauce and stir over high heat until mixture boils, thickens and clears. Makes about 2½ cups.

BEACHCOMBER SUPPER CLUB

5710 Fulton Road, Canton, Ohio

In 1964, there was definitely a tropical charm at the Beachcomber Supper Club in Canton, Ohio. The building's exterior had a mid-century modern design, but its interior was a lush tropical garden. One advertising headline read, "Parties are twice as much fun in the Hawaii of Canton." The Beachcomber was fully decked in Polynesian décor. It had palm trees, tropical plants and the sound of water to add to the ambiance. The business was centrally located downtown and was within walking distance to the Canal Fulton Theatre. The restaurant's hostess was Shirley Null, who guaranteed a wonderful evening. The head chef was Rebert Rohr, who prepared both Continental and American cuisine with tropical flair. There was nightly entertainment inside the cocktail lounge from organ and piano player Jack Heagy. On Friday and Saturday nights, Latin entertainment was provided by the Fabulous Delcos, masters of the rumba and samba. The bar was beautifully surrounded in bamboo and had unique lighting structures overhead. The drink menu was full of unusual and exotic drinks like the Mai Tai, but the bartenders also served their own cocktail: the Beachcomber Pineapple Passion, which was served in a whole pineapple. At some point, the restaurant was sold and reopened as the Trade Winds. This lasted until July 1983, when the restaurant again changed hands and reverted to the original name of the Beachcomber Restaurant. At this point, the restaurant's focus was on seafood, and its Polynesian décor was replaced by red velvet drapes, white tablecloths and a huge crystal chandelier. The property is currently a Winking Lizard Tavern.

KAHONA CLUB

Eastgate Shopping Center, Mansfield-Ashland Road, Mansfield, Ohio

The Kahona Club is the most famous Tiki resort and health spa that was never built. According to a 1966 article in the *News-Journal*, applications for charter memberships in a new Kahona Club, which was advertised as "Ohio's most sensational private club," were being accepted. The advertisement goes on to say that the construction of the club was dependent upon the interest shown and the number of memberships sold. The cost of the proposed club was $468,000, and the estimated size of its one-story building was sixteen thousand square feet. The president of the proposed club would have been Gene Kindinger, who was also the president and treasurer of Charvid Construction Co. Inc., the developers of the Eastgate Shopping Center. A total of 450 family memberships were required for the club to be built. Those who were interested were asked to sign an undated, one-year membership application and include a check that covered one month of the annual dues. In a letter to prospective members, Kindinger said these checks would be held in a special escrow account by the First National Bank. If the goal of 450 memberships was not reached by June 15, 1966, all the checks would be returned. Family memberships were priced at $285 a year, and single memberships were priced at $150 a year.

According to the announced plans, the club would provide a "Hawaiian atmosphere the year round." The club's advertisements exclaimed it would have an exotic Polynesian room with dancing at the Hula Hoi, sauna baths, an Aloha game room, exercise rooms, the Ho-Lo-Koo Apparel Shop, a luau dining room, the Oh-Ah-Hoo Cocktail Lounge and the Ha-Eh-Na Outdoor Pool and Sun Deck. Alas, the Kahona Club was never more than a Polynesian pipe dream.

HOLIDAY INN HAWAIIAN LUAU (TWO LOCATIONS)

Chillicothe, and Zanesville, Ohio

The national chain of Holiday Inn was quick to cash in on the sudden Hawaiian craze that swept the nation in the 1960s and 1970s. Every weekend, the hotel chain would advertise authentic Hawaiian luaus, which included live entertainment and all-you-can-eat buffets.

THE ISLANDER

1650 State Road, Cuyahoga Falls, Ohio

The building at 1650 State Road was formerly part of a Polynesian restaurant called the Islander, but it has been used as a storage facility by the current owner for the past six years. The building was gutted at time of its last purchase and has been left in that condition. It is next to the Golden Dragon Chinese restaurant.

PULLMAN LANES TIKI LOUNGE

3105 OH-103, Willard, Ohio

Pullman Lanes and Tiki Lounge is still in business and currently run as Dynasty Lanes. There are no Tikis in sight, but the lounge does have an End of Summer Luau in September, where Hawaiian attire is strongly encouraged.

SOUTH PACIFIC

2716 Lincoln Way East, Massillon, Ohio

The South Pacific restaurant in Massillon celebrated its grand opening in January 1976. At this time, the Hawaiian restaurant business was in decline, but owner Man Kit Lee decided to give the Polynesian-themed restaurant a try. Man, who was a cook in his native Hong Kong for fifteen years, prepared all of the restaurant's food. His wife, Mee Ying Lee, was the restaurant's hostess. The restaurant touted "Authentic Polynesian Cuisine" and had specials consisting of a Mongolian barbecue dinner and Japanese teriyaki steak. Man Lee and his wife even fashioned the interior décor themselves using imported bamboo and other Polynesian artifacts.

TAHITI LOUNGE

75 North Paint Street, Chillicothe, Ohio

An advertisement for the Tahiti Restaurant in Chillicothe, Ohio. *Author's collection.*

The Tahiti was a supper club and cocktail lounge with Polynesian décor in downtown Chillicothe. It opened in September 1967 and was owned by Emory Mick, who also operated the Williams Hotel. It boasted an amazing sign at the front entrance that displayed the Tahiti name in large bamboo font flanked by two Tiki heads. The restaurant's advertisements welcomed customers to dine, dance and relax in an exotic atmosphere. The Jim Strouse Trio played during the restaurant's grand opening weekend. The Tahiti lasted until 1982, when the business was sold and its liquor license transferred. The restaurant was later reopened as Shady Sadies Saloon.

TIKI BOWLING LANES AND RESTAURANT

1521 Tiki Lane, Lancaster, Ohio

Tiki restaurants with attached bowling alleys are endlessly fascinating. It's a bizarre clash of cultures that works. When the Tiki Restaurant and Bowling Alley first opened, it was much more Polynesian in style and décor. It was the creation of the building's original owner Dick Byrd, and it opened in 1962. At the time, the street was known as Krouse Road, but it was later renamed Tiki Lane in honor of the business. The restaurant had a Polynesian atmosphere complete with "grass hut" booths, floral print, bamboo on the walls and hanging ball lights. The restaurant was also home to a large aquarium filled with exotic fish, which was built into the wall toward the back of the building. The menu included steaks, seafood and homemade apple pie. The interior of the restaurant used to have painted Tiki torches along the walls heading toward the bowling lanes. A *Lancaster Eagle-Gazette* article from 1962 described the thirty-two-lane alley as "one of the most beautiful, well-equipped" bowling alleys in Ohio.

In 1972, there was a major renovation that included an addition of ten bowling lanes. The alley hosted numerous local, state and national bowling tournaments. In the late 1980s or early 1990s, the new owners did a major remodel, which basically wiped out all of the restaurant's Tiki past. Today, the alley still hosts bowling tournaments and, as a nod to its Tiki past, celebrates an annual luau. The exterior of the building remains unchanged and still has a nice Tiki Lanes sign out front and two large, square tile mosaics with Tikis and torches on it.

TIKI LOUNGE

135 Cherry Valley Road, Newark, Ohio

The Tiki Lounge on the west side of Newark was the creation of Findley B. Chappelear Jr. It opened in July 1966 and was the first A-frame building in the area, which immediately drew customers' attention. The building was small, but it did have enough room to accommodate sixty people on its main floor and balcony. To reach the balcony, customers had to ascend a spiral staircase. From the very beginning, Findley wanted to create a unique Polynesian restaurant with an architectural edge. His father, Findley Chappelear Sr., was a well-respected highway engineer. Findley graduated from Newark High School in 1952 and went on to study architecture at Miami University and Ohio State University. The entire Polynesian-style building was designed and built by Findley, minus its plumbing, wiring and foundation. The rear of the main floor had a horseshoe-shaped bar and tables were lined down the restaurant's sides. Most of the building's interior was finished in wood paneling, Formica and burlap. The *Newark Advocate* reported that "wooden masks would be placed inside and outside of the door" to be "used as decoration throughout the lounge." The *Newark Advocate* also stated that there were "plans for a nine-foot idol at the entrance, outside the building." Whether this materialized or not, I don't know, but nine months later, on April 20, 1967, the Tiki Lounge succumbed to a devastating fire. It started in a waste can behind the bar and caused an estimated $15,000 worth of damage. No reference to the restaurant reopening has ever been found.

WAIKIKI RESTAURANT

2616 State Route 59, Ravenna, Ohio

Owned by restaurateur Peter Hwang, the Waikiki Restaurant was known for years as the Copper Kettle before Hwang tossed out the early American maple furniture and replaced it with cobra chairs and ceremonial masks. Before opening the Waikiki, Hwang previously owned the Peking Restaurant on State Road in Cuyahoga Falls. When asked why a native of the Shantung Province in northern China would build a Polynesian restaurant, Hwang exclaimed, "Because I worked in one and travelled in Hawaii. There weren't any in the Akron area, and I thought that people might like it." The restaurant had two large dining rooms, both decorated with tropical foliage, Tiki masks, seashell lamps, hanging fish nets, lots of bamboo and Oriental lanterns. The restaurant was a clash of two cultures. It had Hawaiian music playing on its sound system while it served Polynesian dishes, steak dinners and appetizers like the Flaming Lazy Susan Appetizer plate. The bar served tropical drinks such as the Mai Tai, Scorpion and Navy Grog.

CEDAR POINT, POLYNESIAN PAVILION AND JUNGLE LARRY'S SAFARI

Sandusky, Ohio

Before the Columbus Zoo had Jack Hanna, Cedar Point had Jungle Larry and Safari Jane, a husband-and-wife team that had their own animal safari and gift shop inside one of the most famous amusement parks in the world. Jungle Larry, whose real name is Lawrence Tetzlaff, was a well-respected zoologist. His wife, Nancy Tetzlaff, was known as Safari Jane. In 1964, the couple opened a small animal farm on the Cedar Point property. By 1965, their operation had expanded, and they opened Safari Island and, later, Jungle Larry's African Safari.

A wonderful picture of Jungle Larry and Safari Jane flanked by two large Tikis inside Safari Island at Cedar Point in Sandusky, Ohio. *Courtesy of Tim Tetzlaff.*

Jungle Larry and Safari Jane in their zebra-painted jungle mobile at Safari Land in Cedar Point. *Courtesy of Tim Tetzlaff.*

According to the official Teztlaff website:

> *Safari Island was a true island. The animals had to be rafted across the first season. The secluded wooded area provided a lush jungle atmosphere for the animals. Over the years, Midwesterners would get an up-close look at larger animals, like zebras, eland, lions, elephants, leopards, pythons, tigers and even wolves. Over the years, the cultural experience also included dancers and musicians from Africa.*

In 1969, the Tetzlaffs found their dream home at Caribbean Gardens in Naples, Florida. The location had a warm, tropical climate that was perfect for the animals. It was a financial challenge to run both operations, but Cedar Point was very successful and helped to finance the Naples location. Larry passed away in 1984, but Nancy and their children were determined to continue his legacy. The attraction lasted until 1994 before the safari was being taken over by roller coasters. For thirty years, the Tetzlaffs entertained

One of the Cedar Point Pavilions on the beach at Cedar Point in Sandusky, Ohio. *Courtesy of Scott Schell.*

millions of guests inside their lush tropical jungle. It's interesting to note that the current Speed Zone Gift Shop is the same building that housed the Safari Gift Shop. Today, Cedar Point is still a world-wide tourist destination for coaster enthusiasts, but it is devoid of any of its jungle-related past. For more information on Jungle Larry, visit www.junglelarry.com.

HAWAIIAN PUNCH VILLAGE

Sea World of Ohio, Aurora, Ohio

SeaWorld of Ohio was a theme park and marine zoological park located in Aurora, Ohio. The park was developed by George Millay, founder of the SeaWorld brand, and Earl Gascoigne, who had recently left Cedar Point to redevelop the struggling amusement park called Geauga Lake. The Ohio SeaWorld project was announced in 1968, and its name was changed to SeaWorld Cleveland when it opened to the public on May 29, 1970. It was the second SeaWorld park to be built in the chain following SeaWorld San Diego, which opened six years earlier. The marine park was beautifully landscaped and included hundreds of trees, shrubs and a rich assortment of vegetation. The Hawaiian Village opened in 1971 and was a unique area that featured carved Tikis and fine Polynesian dining.

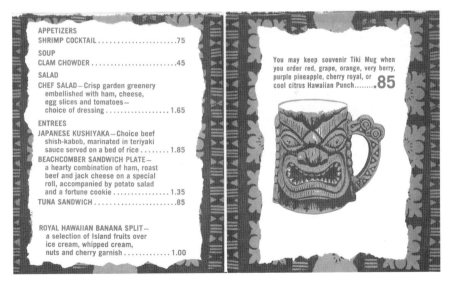

A menu for a restaurant inside the Hawaiian Punch Village at Sea World in Aurora, Ohio. *Courtesy of Scott Schell.*

ALOHA RESTAURANT

1212 Youngstown-Warren Road, Niles, Ohio

The Aloha Restaurant changed hands and became the Sunshine Buffet. The beautiful, small A-frame structure is still there, but it appears to have been abandoned.

WAIKIKI RESTAURANT

2351 Columbus Avenue NE., Canton, Ohio

This was a second Waikiki location that was also owned by Peter Hwang. It closed in 1976.

BAMBOO HOUSE

1234 North Court Street, Circleville, Ohio 43113

The Bamboo House was owned and managed by a former staffer of the Diamond Head restaurant in Chillicothe.

OTHER OHIO TIKI RESTAURANTS

Chung's Restaurant
21080 Lorain Road, Fairview Park, Ohio

Bali-Hai
128 West Boardman Street, Youngstown, Ohio (next to City Hall)

The Beachcomber
3523 Manchester Road, Akron, Ohio

A close-up view of a Tiki mug that was specifically made for Chung's Restaurant in Fairview Park, Ohio. *Courtesy of Scott Schell.*

Puki Puki
Old Troy Pike, Huber Heights, Ohio

Rattan Room
Warren, Ohio

Surf Lounge
2112 Cleveland Road, Sandusky, Ohio

South Pacific
Lyndhurst, Ohio

Tahiti Restaurant
27026 Center Ridge Road, Westlake, Ohio

Tiki Dairy Queen
1779 Stringtown Road, Grove City, Ohio 43123

7

KAHIKI MEMORIES

Most people from Ohio know about the legendary Kahiki Supper Club. Since a book on the Kahiki has already been written (The History Press, 2015), I chose to include some interviews with the people who were instrumental in its illustrious history. I interviewed the Kahiki's original owner, Bill Sapp, at length about the restaurant and the tough decision he made to sell it in the 1970s. Gerline Lude was a familiar face at the Kahiki, and she served as a waitress and, occasionally, a mystery girl during the restaurant's early years. Her stories and memories from that time play an important part in understanding what it was like to work at such a prestigious supper club. When the Kahiki announced it was closing in 2000, Tiki pioneer and archaeologist Otto von Stroheim decided that if he couldn't save the restaurant, he would at least throw the biggest closing party ever. Together with Michael Tsao, Stroheim planned the "Bon Voyage, Kahiki" party.

BILL SAPP

Tiki Pioneer and Original Owner of the Kahiki Supper Club

In 1961, Bill Sapp and Lee Henry opened one of the most magnificent and visually stunning Polynesian restaurants in the world: the Kahiki Supper Club in Columbus, Ohio. More than just a restaurant, the Kahiki was a

Above: A young Bill Sapp with his friends on vacation. *Courtesy of Linda Sapp-Long.*

Right: Beachboy Bill Sapp playing the ukulele. *Courtesy of Linda Sapp-Long.*

classic example of mid-century Polynesian Pop architecture and one of Bill's most creative endeavors. Although the restaurant was demolished in 2000 to make way for a Walgreen's, it has reached cult status among many urban archaeologists and Tikiphiles around the world.

Bill and Lee, college buddies who met while attending Ohio State University, opened the Top Steakhouse in 1955. This successful venture sparked Bill's imagination. He was keenly aware that the new state of Hawaii and the popularity of the film *South Pacific* had ignited a nationwide craze. Polynesian restaurants like the Mai-Kai, Trader Vic's and Don the Beachcomber's were doing brisk business. In 1959, Bill and Lee opened the Grass Shack, a small thatched bungalow on the east side of Columbus, as an experiment to determine how a Polynesian-style restaurant would work in Ohio. The Grass Shack had good business, but it mysteriously burned down on June 14, 1959—Bill's birthday.

Bill and Lee wanted to rebuild the restaurant, but they wanted something more on the scale of the Mai-Kai in Fort Lauderdale. Loren M. Berry, Lee's father-in-law, guaranteed a loan to begin construction in 1960. The architects of the Kahiki's building were Ralph Sounik and Ned Eller of Design Associates. Coburn Morgan was hired as the decorator. Coburn, the original designer, Bernie Altenbach and Bill conceived and designed the giant Moai fireplace. Coburn designed the garden area and oversaw the placement of the Polynesian décor. After nine months of construction, the total cost for building the restaurant came out to just over a million dollars. The Kahiki Supper Club officially opened its doors in February 1961.

I met Bill Sapp in 2007 while I was writing for *Tiki Magazine*. Bill was still interested in the restaurant business and was getting ready to open up an Italian sandwich shop in Bexley. It was there that I conducted this interview.

> *JEFF CHENAULT. How did you meet Lee Henry?*
>
> *BILL SAPP. We went to college together at Ohio State, and we were roommates. We would hang out at different places downtown and talk about the bar and restaurant business. I had been in the restaurant business for a short time in Florida. I told Lee I thought it was a great business, so we got together and looked at different restaurants. We went out to the Top Steakhouse; at that time, it was just a little beer joint. We transformed it over a year or so into what it is today.*
>
> *JEFF. The Kahiki started as the Grass Shack. What year did it open?*
>
> *BILL. In 1959, we were looking for a location to put a Polynesian restaurant, and the Grass Shack was it. So, we bought the land and opened*

Bill Sapp (*left*) and Lee Henry (*right*) on opening day, in February 1961, of the Kahiki in Columbus, Ohio. *Author's collection.*

the Grass Shack. Sandro Conti, who made all the drinks and everything, managed and operated the Grass Shack. It was a real success. It enabled us to use the materials that we used in the Kahiki, because it burned down after my birthday party one night. The fire marshal at the time wasn't going to allow us to build the Grass Shack with all the grass thatch and everything. We had to put a product called Flame-Art from California on all the grass. The only thing that didn't burn when the Grass Shack burned down was the stuff we put the Flame-Art on.

After my party, I went home. It was about 4:00 in the morning when I left. I got home, and about an hour later, Sandro called and said, "Bill, we got fire down here." I said, "Well, put it out. I'll see you tomorrow." An hour after that, he called again. "Bill, this is a pretty good fire." I said, "Sandro, will we be able to open in the morning?" "Well, maybe" he said. Another hour goes by, and he called again and said, "Hey, Bill, ain't no Grass Shack."

JEFF. How did you meet Sandro Conti?

BILL. I met Sandro sometime before that at the Top Steakhouse. It was on a Sunday evening. I had been tending bar and, at that time, according to the law, you could only sell whiskey until midnight on Sunday. Another bar owner from Pataskala and I were the only ones sitting at the bar, and this long-haired, blue-eyed guy came in the door. I was tired from playing golf all day, so I said, in Spanish under my breath, "If you want a drink, go make your own," and he walked right back to the bar and said, "Si, commena," and mixed himself a drink. It turns out, he's Italian and lived, until he was eleven years old, in Italy. His family moved, through a political appointment–type thing, to Nicaragua. He grew up in Nicaragua and was fluent in both Italian and Spanish, and then, he came to the United States in either 1958 or 1959. When he came into The Top that night, he could say "hello," and that was the extent of his English. We talked Spanish all the time, and that's how we became very good friends.

JEFF. What inspired you to build the Kahiki?

BILL. Well, we were doing pretty good. We had The Top restaurant going from 1955 until about 1959, and we decided, "You know, let's open another restaurant. This one is okay, but two would be better." So, Lee Henry and I traveled around the country, and we would check out all the different restaurants. We found that Trader Vic's and the Mai Kai were doing great when other restaurants were not doing so good. We decided to build one of our own Polynesian restaurants here in Columbus.

JEFF. What was the cost, and how long did it take to build?

BILL. At that time, it cost a little over a million dollars to build and took about a year to complete.

JEFF. When did the Kahiki open, and how did you come up with the Kahiki name?

BILL. The Kahiki opened in 1961. I got the name out of a Polynesian dictionary. I just went through it and looked at all the different names. Kahiki means "to sail to Tahiti" in Polynesian vernacular.

JEFF. Who was Coburn Morgan, and who hired him to design and decorate the Kahiki?

BILL. Well, the original designer was not Coburn, it was Bernie Altenbach. Bernie came up with the idea of the Polynesian meeting house, and he got it started and it was well on its way. Coburn Morgan came in as the decorator. Bernie Altenbach designed the different rooms inside the Kahiki but never really got the credit that he deserved. Bernie had just

An early picture of Sandro Conti and a friend at one of Bill's parties. *Courtesy of Linda Sapp-Long.*

finished remodeling the Top at that time. We hired Bernie to do it, but when he got too busy, he had Coburn take over. Coburn Morgan was very outgoing and got all the credit.

JEFF. Where did you get the stuff to fill the Kahiki, and whose idea was the giant fireplace?

BILL. Most of the stuff Lee and I got out of Florida. All the building materials and everything came from people in Florida who were importing things at the time. The fireplace and the two giant Moai outside were a combination of Bernie, Coburn and me. Everybody always seemed to come up with an idea, and if it sounded good, we went with it.

JEFF. Who named all the different rooms inside the Kahiki?

BILL. Everybody seemed to help out. We put the outrigger canoe in the bar, so we called it the Outrigger Bar. Either Coburn or Lee came up with the Quiet Village name, but I really don't remember who.

JEFF. Were there any plans for the Kahiki that never came to light? Like, maybe a hula revue or some big-name acts?

BILL. No, we never had any plans for that, but we did have some musicians play occasionally. We had one guy named Marsh Padilla who was playing there almost every night, and he seemed to be a satisfying musician. We never really needed to get into a revue like they do at the Mai Kai. We figured that we wanted to attract local customers, mostly because the Mai Kai had a steady stream of visiting customers. In Columbus, Ohio, you really didn't get that.

JEFF. Do you recall any famous people that visited the Kahiki.

BILL. Oh, many! The Kenley Players were based in Columbus, and they had a deal that after all the plays, they would all come to the Kahiki. I remember Ann Margaret, Barbara Eden and Arthur Godfrey—all kinds of stars. The one that really impressed me was the guy that played in The Lost Weekend, Ray Milland. He was really a down-to-earth, nice guy. I was sitting in the office doing some bookwork, and he just wandered upstairs and was looking all around, and my door was open. He just walked in and said, "Hey, how are you doing?" I said, "Fine, how are you?" He said, "Oh, I'm doing great. You know, you really got a nice place here. I really enjoyed it." I said, "Well, sit down, and let's talk about it." He sat down, and we talked for two hours. I never did know who he was until he started to leave, and I said, "By the way, what's your name?" He said, "Ray Milland." He was really a big star back then.

JEFF. With the initial success of the Kahiki, did you ever consider opening another location or a smaller Kahiki's?

BILL. Not in the first year. We never even thought about it. We were so tired from all this and the way it went over and everything. We were making money like we never dreamed of. We really didn't think of any others. At one time, though, after we had been open a year, we got a call from some people in Hawaii who wanted us to open over there, but we didn't. We thought about that pretty seriously, but in the meantime, we were working on plans to open a Kahiki in Cincinnati. We applied for a liquor license and did everything down there, but we were never able to make any kind of deal for a lot down there, so it just fell through.

JEFF. It must have been a lot of work just to keep the Kahiki going.

BILL. Sandro and I flew down to Miami and stayed at the Columbus Hotel for about three weeks, and we hired mostly Cuban refugees. I would say that 75 percent of the people that opened the Kahiki were Cuban refugees. There were doctors, lawyers, musicians and everything. They came up here and worked very diligently. They were great workers. One of the men was a physician in Cuba and got licensed here, and it turned out, he helped deliver my daughter! The Cubans are great people. They are very industrious people full of rhythm. They love to dance.

JEFF. I heard you and Sandro went down to Cuba together.

BILL. Well, Sandro and I went on one of our regular junkets to Cuba, which we did often because we had so much fun down there. We stayed in the "old" section of Havana, because that's where we liked it the most. Sandro and I were going out. My wife was tired, so she said, "I'm going to stay in the room." Sandro and I go out. . . . This is when the revolution was going on, so the revolutionaries started storming "old" Havana, shooting and everything. Sandro and I were in some bar, and we wanted to go to another bar, and we didn't care about any damn revolutionaries. So, we went out and hailed a cab, and this cab stopped but he said, "I ain't taking you anyplace, I'm afraid that they'll kill me." Sandro said, "If you don't take us where we want to go, we're going to kill you right now!" So, he took us to this other bar where we stayed for a while. Anyway, the sun started to rise, so I'm thinking the wife's going to be furious. We get back to the hotel, and there's an iron gate there, and we can't get in. So, we rattled this gate for an hour. Finally, the caretaker comes, because he thinks the revolutionaries are trying to break in. We assured him that we were tourists and guests of the hotel, so he finally let us in. Well, we get into the hotel, and the elevator doesn't work. We were up on the eleventh floor, so we went up the stairs and, by the time we got to the room, we were both just beat. So, anyway, I went in and went to bed. The next morning, my wife screamed "Bill, Bill get up." I said, "What's the matter?" She said, "Look at this." I looked out the window, and they had hung somebody down there, and he was swinging in the breeze. My wife said, "Let's get out of here." We decided it was best to get out of there, so we changed our reservations and got on the last plane out of there. Just as we were taking off, we got up and immediately dropped back down from Havana to Vera Dera Beach, the airport there. Some guys had gone down the canal and were shooting machine guns, or something,

A rare shot of Bill Sapp, Sandro Conti and a friend in Havana, Cuba. *Courtesy of Linda Sapp-Long.*

and the pilots were afraid they were going to shoot the plane out of the air. There were some people, I guess, on the plane that shouldn't have been there, so they lined us all up and poked us with guns and searched everything. Everybody was scared. Finally, we were able to get back on the plane, and we took off for Miami.

JEFF. Who was J.J. Hite?

BILL. He made various ceramic products for the Kahiki. My wife at the time was very instrumental in designing and making ceramics, so she and Jack worked together on various drink vessels. They were made in the basement of the Kahiki. Almost all of the mugs that were made out of clay were made by my wife and Jack. These were made before Hoffman Pottery.

We didn't get into buying that commercial stuff at the time, because there wasn't any money until we really got going. The Hoffman stuff came later. There was probably only about 25 Mystery Bowls made because they broke fairly easy. They were subject to being stolen too.

JEFF: Didn't the Kahiki have a garden area outside?

BILL: Yes, when we first opened. All the items that were in the garden area were items we got from a company in Florida, and we had them shipped up here. I've still got the one I liked the best at my house. We also brought palm trees up from Florida—natural palm trees. On opening night, I was sitting at a table with my mother and a party of people, when a little green snake dropped down out of the palm tree and onto our table. It scared my mother to death!

JEFF: When did you sell the Kahiki, and who did you sell it too?

BILL: We sold it to Mitch Boitch in 1976, I believe. Mitch leased it to Michael Tsao. After a couple of years, Michael made an offer to buy it from him over a period of time.

JEFF: Michael Tsao came from Trader Vic's in Los Angeles, right?

BILL: Yes, that's how he got in there, because Mitch ran into him one time at Trader Vic's in Los Angeles and was impressed by him.

JEFF: Tell us about the time you were up in the office and got robbed.

BILL: I'd been playing in a golf tournament in Dayton, and I came back. There were back stairs at the Kahiki that led to the offices. So, I came up the stairs, walked in the back door and walked into my office, and there were two guys in there. I thought they were working on the fish tank over my safe in the office. Then, all of a sudden, I'm looking at a gun. They said, "We need you to open the safe." I said, "Hell, I can't open the safe. I don't even know the combination." They said, "Well, who does?" I said, "The only one I know that does is the secretary, and she's not here." So, he said, "You get her on the phone and get that combination, or something's going to happen to you like the guy last night." There was a robbery the night before, and they shot the guy. I didn't know that at the time, so it didn't bother me. Anyway, I called the secretary up, she gave me the combination and I opened the safe for them. There was a couple thousand dollars in it. When they left, they wired me up and, as an afterthought, took the money I had on me, which pissed me off. I had won a money clip in that tournament over there. I said, "Hey, leave me that money clip. I just won it in a golf tournament." He said, "Okay," and gave it back to me.

GERLINE LUDE

An Interview with a Mystery Girl

I first met Geri when her daughter Tracy saw a picture of the Beachcomber Trio album on Facebook. I helped produce the album for Dionysus Records back in 2010. Tracy sent me a message and said, "I think that's my mother on your album cover." Indeed, it was, and I was shocked to learn that she was still living in Columbus, Ohio. Tracy put me in touch with her mom, and I discovered that it, indeed, was her. We have been friends ever since. The first thing I noticed when visiting her house was that her entire backyard was decorated like a huge Polynesian village. There were fountains, a swimming pool, banana plants, tropical flowers and a Japanese-style gazebo that doubled as a cocktail bar. I learned later that she had won multiple awards from the Columbus Home and Garden Show and was featured in various gardening magazines. She was obviously influenced by the tropical décor of the world-famous Kahiki restaurant, and it showed in everything she did. I also found out that Geri is an avid bird fan. At the time of this interview, she had a total of nine birds, including two macaws, a couple of cockatoos and a lot of parrots.

This interview was conducted at the home of Jack and Geri Lude in 2010.

JEFF CHENAULT. When did you start working at the Kahiki?

GERLINE LUDE. I started working there in 1962. I was twenty years old when I started there, and I wasn't old enough to serve drinks. I started as a hostess, then became a waitress. I was also a Mystery Girl for a couple of years.

JEFF. I heard the waitresses all had to wear dark-colored wigs.

GERLINE. Yes, all the waitresses had to wear wigs. Back in those days, the poofier, the better! Originally, I tried darkening my hair, but it wasn't dark enough. They were always on me about my hair, and I thought, "I'm getting tired of wearing these stupid wigs!"

JEFF. What was it like to work there?

GERLINE. Oh, it was a lot of fun—so many good memories. Merrick "Chills" Vern was our manager at the time. He originally worked at Mario's International before coming to the Kahiki. I remember the gong that was used for the Mystery Girl was so huge, it would just echo, echo and echo constantly. It would never stop ringing. The tables were all numbered, and they had little huts you would go into. The Rainforest Room was on the

Jack and Gerline Lude in their backyard tropical paradise. *Author's collection.*

right, and the fish tanks were on the left. Down the middle, behind the big waterfall, you came to an area with a big round table. I'll never forget the name, table #51. That's where all the Kenley Players used to dine.

JEFF. Did you get to meet any of the stars?

GERLINE. Oh my, I had so many pictures taken with so many stars back then. I just loved Robert Stack from The Untouchables. *George Hamilton was really nice. Also, Robert Goulet, Ray Milland and Zsa Zsa Gabor were there a lot.*

JEFF. Where was the gong located back then?

GERLINE. When you walked past the maître d' stand, the piano bar was on the left. On the other side of the piano bar there was a hallway where the Mystery Girl would come out. Just before you entered that area, back toward the service bar, the big gong was hanging on the wall. Everybody stopped and looked when that gong went off, because it was a big deal when that Mystery Girl came out.

JEFF. How did you serve the Mystery Bowl?

GERLINE. When we would serve the Mystery drink, we would carry the drink out, we would walk in front of table #51, and we would first present the drink to the big Tiki god fireplace, kneel down on one knee and back up again. Then, we would bring the drink to the customer. We also had a lei that we would place over their head, and if the customer was a man, I would usually kiss him on the forehead.

JEFF. Do you remember the photo shoot for the picture used on the Beachcomber Trio album?

GERLINE. Yes, I'd been working there for a little while, so it was around 1963 or 1964.

JEFF. Charles Moore was the photographer; do you remember him?

GERLINE. Not really. They just set everything up and told us what to do and where to stand. I had my big wig on for that shot.

JEFF. Do you remember Marsh Padilla?

GERLINE. Oh, yes, I remember Marsh very well. Everybody loved Marsh. He was so talented and could play so many different instruments.

JEFF. When the band wasn't playing, was there music playing in the background?

GERLINE. There was always music playing. The band usually played from 8:00 p.m. to 1:00 a.m. After that, the music was pumped in from a big reel-to-reel that, I think, was upstairs in the office. The controls were over by the maître d' stand. It was mostly Hawaiian-style music.

JEFF. Do you have any other fond memories?

GERLINE. I remember they had a big toucan bird upstairs in the offices named George, and every day, I would come up and bring some fruit for him. He would come up to the cage and let me rub his beak. He was a great bird.

I also remember they had a little pottery shop downstairs in the basement. They would make things like ashtrays…and sell them in the Beachcomber Shop. Back then, they sold some really nice stuff—quality stuff that you didn't see later on.

It was just a fun place to work—some of the best years of my life!

Geri held an annual Kahiki Luau party in her backyard for years. It was a party that celebrated everything that the Kahiki embodied: friends, food, drink and a true love for a famous Polynesian restaurant.

THE "BON VOYAGE, KAHIKI" PARTY

August 26, 2000, Columbus, Ohio

When word had spread that the Kahiki was being sold in early 2000, people from all over the United States came to visit the restaurant one last time. Being a local, I visited the Kahiki as much as my wallet would allow. It was inconceivable to me that a restaurant with so much history and grandeur could be torn down. It was in the National Register of Historic Places for goodness's sake. But, when the rumors turned into facts, it really sunk in. I had talked to Michael Tsao about the closing, and he was reassuring about wanting to reopen the Kahiki. Michael told me he was working with the City of Columbus to secure a spot on the Scioto River for a new Kahiki. I even saw an artist's rendition of the new building. I had my doubts, but I think that Michael's heart was truly sincere in wanting to rebuild.

Otto von Stroheim had been publishing *Tiki News* since 1996, documenting the burgeoning Tiki culture revival that was on the horizon. When Otto found out that the Kahiki was sold and going to close, he talked to Michael Tsao about throwing the "Bon Voyage, Kahiki" party. He agreed, and the plans were made to throw the biggest Tiki party ever.

The entertainers were lined up, and a ten-piece band from Hawaii called Don Tiki was scheduled to headline. This party was a monumental feat with all the logistics involved. The emcee for the evening was the fun-loving King Kukulele, also known as Denny Moynehan. The King had an uncanny ability to make people laugh. With his grass skirt, ukulele and infectious personality, he was the perfect choice. The actual feast was held in the basement of the Kahiki. It was the biggest spread of food I had ever seen. For entertainment, they hired big-time lounge and exotica DJs from all over the country to spin records while people dined on an incredible Hawaiian Luau buffet. I was one of the DJs that Otto invited, because I had a great love of exotica music, especially Les Baxter. The other DJs included Jack Fetterman of New York, Michael Toth of Akron, Ohio, and James Botticelli from Boston.

Mark Gunderson was the sound man for the main entertainment. Instruments and amplifiers were set up in the dining room, and the main stage circled around the giant Tiki god fireplace. Otto had even convinced Martin Denny, the king of exotica music, to attend the event, but he eventually backed out due to health concerns. Lloyd Kendall filmed a video of Martin Denny to explain why he couldn't attend and to thank everyone for inviting him; then, Martin started playing "Quiet Village" on the piano. While he

A Bon Voyage, Kahiki postcard with artwork by Dirty Donny. *Author's collection.*

was playing, the Don Tiki ensemble started playing "Quiet Village" as well, in sync with Mr. Denny. It was perfectly timed, and the magical transition from video tape to the real band was simply breathtaking. With this video, the party had officially begun.

It was an evening of celebration and sadness. John Holt documented a lot of the evening on video. At the end of the night, King Kukulele and I left together, since he was staying at my house. As we entered the car, it started to rain. We looked at each other, and Denny said, "The Tiki gods are crying." I will never forget that moment. Denny, and a lot of other people I met that night, have a bond and friendship that still lingers today.

Otto von Stroheim recalled the event:

Monumental and historic: those are two words that describe the Kahiki restaurant and the closing party that Tiki News *produced there on August 26, 2000. Words cannot describe the overwhelming architecture and the perfect Polynesian and Tiki ambience of the Kahiki. Nor can mere words begin to describe the warmth, hospitality and goodwill that abounded within the walls of Kahiki when five hundred Tiki lovers converged there for its farewell party.*

Upon hearing rumors that Walgreen's had purchased the Kahiki, I called owner turned CEO Michael Tsao directly. In our first conversation, he said he could not comment but assured, "You will be the first to know if I sell the Kahiki." A month later, after the contract was signed, Michael phoned. "I called you even before I talked to my wife!" At that point, Michael told me of his intent to reopen the Kahiki in a more desirable locale (he had already spent a lot of money developing plans and proposals to send to the City of Columbus). He asked for my support for this move and for my help in throwing the best Tiki party I could imagine. Right from the start, Michael was very generous, very honest and very supportive of my concept for the closing party. I took care of most of the initial publicity work, because, as Michael said, "I am not into PR. You do that. We put our heads down and keep working." That's exactly what Michael and Alice Tsao did for four months straight, right up until the end of the "Bon Voyage, Kahiki" party.

As the party took off, the Kahiki house band gave the guests upstairs a taste of what a typical Saturday night at the Kahiki was like. This was anything but a typical night, as master chef in the making (and Michael's son) Jeff Tsao orchestrated a top-of-the-line luau, with huge shrimp skewers pinned into towers made from fresh pineapples, two full roasted pigs

Above, from left to right: This book's author, Jeff Chenault, Bob Brooks and Otto von Stroheim at the Bon Voyage, Kahiki party. *Courtesy of Otto von Stroheim.*

Left: Kahiki owner Michael Tsao (*left*) with *Tiki News* publisher Otto von Stroheim (*right*) during the closing party of the Kahiki Supper Club. *Courtesy of Otto von Stroheim.*

Sven Kirsten and Otto von Stroheim with a copy of *The Book of Tiki* during the Bon Voyage, Kahiki party. *Author's collection.*

with candied cherries for eyes, salmon paté shaped like a large salmon, a make-your-own wonton bar and lots of vegetarian fare. Jeff was attending culinary school in Boston and took two months off to work the closing days of the Kahiki.

It was a full weekend of exotica for those who were anxious to partake. On Friday, there was a performance from the Michael Toth–led Exotic Akron Tour, and on Sunday, a luau was thrown by locals Hoffa, Dana, Jimmy, and Elise.

As the décor was packed up and the Kahiki's birds and fish were donated to a local school, I was reminded of the important work of local reporter Joe Blundo, who broke the story of Kahiki's impending doom for the Columbus Dispatch *in April 2000. He continued to keep the story in the international eye and on the local front page.*

The Kahiki's closing party was part dream and part nightmare for me. While it was a dream come true to be a major player in possibly the biggest Tiki event of the year, if not the decade, it was alternately depressing to think that one of the world's best Tiki bars would soon meet its demise and that I was basically powerless to stop it.

The entertainment lineup for the Bon Voyage, Kahiki Party. *Author's collection.*

For this author, it was a magical evening that I will never forget. Sven Kirsten was celebrating his birthday and the release of his new book called *The Book of Tiki*. It was published by Taschen Books in 2000 and was instrumental in kicking off the entire Tiki resurgence. After the party, Otto went on to start the Tiki Oasis event, first in Palm Springs and then in San Diego. A year later, Christie White started the Hukilau event in Fort Lauderdale, Florida. Both events are still going strong to this day and sell out every year.

8

TIKI MUSIC

Music has always played an important role in Tiki bars. It sets the mood and atmosphere and brings everything together. If a Tiki bar plays the wrong music, it can destroy the atmosphere that the bar is trying to create. Without the correct music, it's just another bar. It would be like a Tiki bar with no Tikis or bamboo—it doesn't work. Authentic Hawaiian music with steel guitars or sophisticated exotica music with Latin rhythms, primitive percussion and birdcalls work best. Lately, a lot of newer Tiki bars have started playing surf music, which works to an extent but moves away from the escapism of exotica.

MARSH PADILLA

Bandleader for the Beachcomber Trio

Marcel "Marsh" Padilla was born on January 16, 1918, in Mexico. His family immigrated to the United States in the 1920s, and that is when he began to study the saxophone and clarinet as a child. Over time, he became a master of the tenor saxophone, alto saxophone, flute, clarinet, guitar, piano, bass guitar, marimba and congas. At fourteen, he moved to Topeka, Kansas, and began playing in local bands. He joined Juan Rodrigo's band out of El Paso in 1936 and moved with them to Detroit two years later. Marsh subsequently

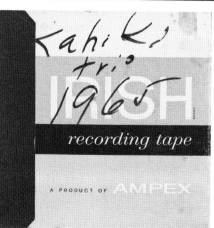

Above: Marsh Padilla plays the flute while an unknown friend plays percussion. *Author's collection*.

Left: The lost Beachcomber Trio reel, which was eventually released on vinyl by Dionysus Records in 2010. *Author's collection*.

played with many bands throughout the Midwest. During World War II, Marsh served as the lead saxophone player for the Camp Roberts Band, which backed the likes of Judy Garland, Martha Raye, Bing Crosby and Bob Hope. After the war, he returned to Detroit to organize the Marcel Padilla Orchestra at the Famous Door and Haig's Supper Club.

In 1958, he came to Columbus from Detroit and led the Beachcomber Trio at the Kahiki from 1961 to 1978. Marsh also worked at the Clifford Hotel, Neil House, Deshler Hotel and Valley Dale. For a time, he toured with Bob Crosby's band as a tenor saxophone player. Aside from becoming a barber and operating his own salon with his wife, Nina, he also taught woodwinds at Coyle Music. Marsh officially retired in 1998 but not before recording an album with local artist Anna Greer—but that's another story. The following year, Marsh was inducted into the Columbus Senior Musicians Hall of Fame.

In 2009, Marsh and Nina retired to Boise, Idaho, to be closer to family. During the move, Marsh found three seven-inch-reels of the Beachcomber Trio that were recorded inside the Kahiki in 1965. The boxes were marked "The Kahiki Trio." Marsh had no recollection of these recordings or who may have recorded them. He gave them to me, and Lee Joseph, of Dionysus Records, released the *Beachcomber Trio Live at the Kahiki* album in 2010. A few months later, Marsh passed away, but he was humbled and honored to see his music released after forty-five years.

JEFF CHENAULT INTERVIEW WITH MARSH PADILLA

This interview was conducted at the home of Marsh and Nina Padilla in Columbus, Ohio, in 2008.

> *JEFF CHENAULT. The Kahiki was inspired by the Mai Kai in Fort Lauderdale. They had a Mystery Girl as well.*
>
> *MARSH PADILLA. They stole a lot of ideas from them, no question. Coburn Morgan also had a lot of great ideas.*
>
> *JEFF. Did you also know "Chills" Vern?*
>
> *MARSH. Oh, yes, he was the maître d'. He first started out as a waiter, then bartender and then maître d'. He did alright. His father had a bar… in the shopping center across the street from the Kahiki.*
>
> *JEFF. Wasn't the Desert Inn across the street?*

MARSH. Yes, on the left. The shopping center was on the right. An Italian family, the Alexanders, owned the Desert Inn. They also owned Little Italy and the Palm Garden. I also knew the bartenders, Bob Karst and Tommy Joseph, pretty well. They started out the same way, as waiters, and then worked their way up to bartender. Johnny Gim worked in the kitchen, tended bar and later became an assistant manager.

While looking through Sven Kirsten's *Book of Tiki*, Marsh commented, "All these places made money." It was here that Marsh recognized the man in the white jacket in one of the Beachcomber Trio pictures.

MARSH. That's "Chills" Vern right there. I think his first name was Merrick. Funny name for an Italian. The photographer pulled other people together to take the picture. He lives in Arizona now.

I remember one day, a French newspaper sent a girl reporter to interview different people—bartenders, me and management—for an article back in Paris, but I never saw the article.

One of my musicians committed suicide while I was there, in the parking lot of the Top restaurant. [He was a] wonderful musician. I think it was Roger Wolf. He was the drummer.

Do you remember Bob Crosby? He was the youngest of the Crosbys.

JEFF. How did you meet him?

MARSH. Another friend of mine was playing trombone for the band. We toured Wisconsin, Michigan and all over the Midwest until something pulled Bob back to Los Angeles. He had the tour booked, and somebody would always run off on him.

JEFF. Was it a lot of fun playing at the Kahiki?

MARSH. Yes, it was when you had the right people. It was hard to keep the right people. The money wasn't there, and the schedule was pretty tight. We could play anything we wanted. The only limitations were the personnel. We got a new man on guitar, got a new man on the bass. We went through a lot of people, but I stayed there and kept the thing going for eighteen years. Until, finally, we got the word they were going to cut out the music. Oh, God!

JEFF. While playing music at the Kahiki, you didn't play all Hawaiian music?

MARSH. Oh, no. If you had to play Hawaiian music continuously, you'd go out of your mind!

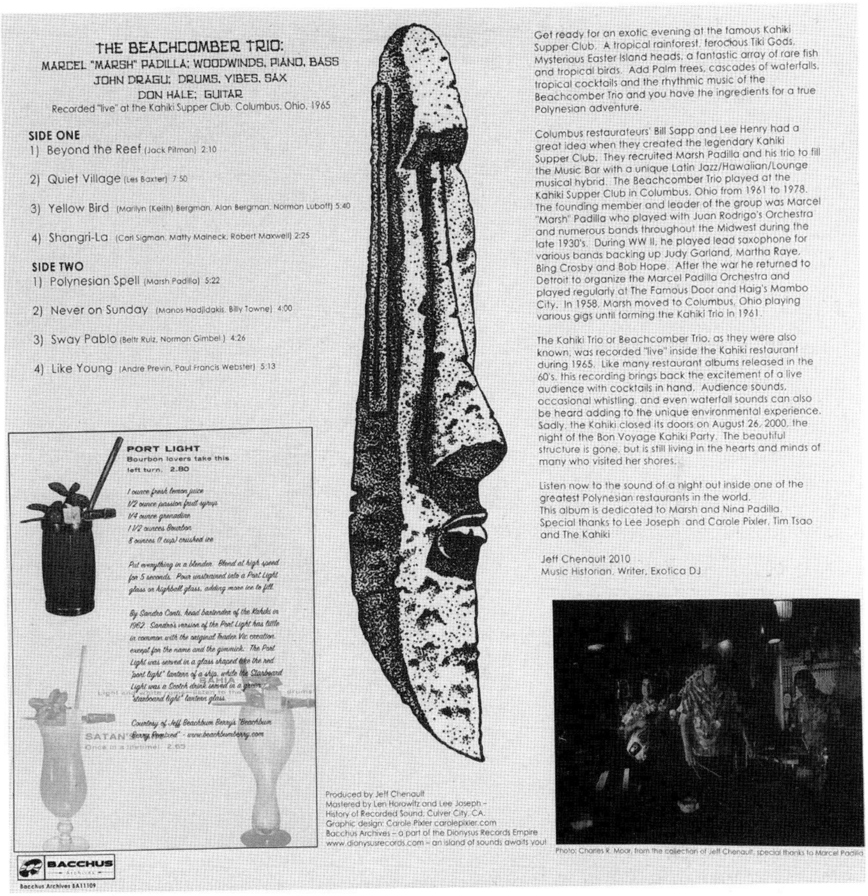
THE BEACHCOMBER TRIO:
MARCEL "MARSH" PADILLA: WOODWINDS, PIANO, BASS
JOHN DRAGU: DRUMS, VIBES, SAX
DON HALE: GUITAR
Recorded "live" at the Kahiki Supper Club, Columbus, Ohio, 1965
SIDE ONE
1) Beyond the Reef (Jack Pitman) 2:10
2) Quiet Village (Les Baxter) 7:50
3) Yellow Bird (Marilyn (Keith) Bergman, Alan Bergman, Norman Luboff) 5:40
4) Shangri-La (Carl Sigman, Matty Malneck, Robert Maxwell) 2:25
SIDE TWO
1) Polynesian Spell (Marsh Padilla) 5:22
2) Never on Sunday (Manos Hadjidakis, Billy Towne) 4:00
3) Sway Pablo (Beltr Ruiz, Norman Gimbel) 4:26
4) Like Young (Andre Previn, Paul Francis Webster) 5:13
PORT LIGHT
Bourbon lovers take this left turn. 2.80
1 ounce fresh lemon juice
1/2 ounce passion fruit syrup
1/4 ounce grenadine
1 1/2 ounces Bourbon
8 ounces (1 cup) crushed ice
Put everything in a blender. Blend at high speed for 5 seconds. Pour unstrained into a Port Light glass or highball glass, adding more ice to fill.
By Sandro Conti, head bartender of the Kahiki in 1962. Sandro's version of the Port Light has little in common with the original Trader Vic creation except for the name and the gimmick. The Port Light was served in a glass shaped like the red "port light" lantern of a ship, while the Starboard Light was a Scotch drink served in a green "starboard light" lantern glass.
Courtesy of Jeff Beachbum Berry's "Beachbum Berry Remixed" - www.beachbumberry.com
Get ready for an exotic evening at the famous Kahiki Supper Club. A tropical rainforest, ferocious Tiki Gods, Mysterious Easter Island heads, a fantastic array of rare fish and tropical birds. Add Palm trees, cascades of waterfalls, tropical cocktails and the rhythmic music of the Beachcomber Trio and you have the ingredients for a true Polynesian adventure.
Columbus restaurateurs' Bill Sapp and Lee Henry had a great idea when they created the legendary Kahiki Supper Club. They recruited Marsh Padilla and his trio to fill the Music Bar with a unique Latin Jazz/Hawaiian/Lounge musical hybrid. The Beachcomber Trio played at the Kahiki Supper Club in Columbus, Ohio from 1961 to 1978. The founding member and leader of the group was Marcel "Marsh" Padilla who played with Juan Rodrigo's Orchestra and numerous bands throughout the Midwest during the late 1930's. During WW II, he played lead saxophone for various bands backing up Judy Garland, Martha Raye, Bing Crosby and Bob Hope. After the war he returned to Detroit to organize the Marcel Padilla Orchestra and played regularly at The Famous Door and Haig's Mambo City. In 1958, Marsh moved to Columbus, Ohio playing various gigs until forming the Kahiki Trio in 1961.
The Kahiki Trio or Beachcomber Trio, as they were also known, was recorded "live" inside the Kahiki restaurant during 1965. Like many restaurant albums released in the 60's, this recording brings back the excitement of a live audience with cocktails in hand. Audience sounds, occasional whistling, and even waterfall sounds can also be heard adding to the unique environmental experience. Sadly, the Kahiki closed its doors on August 26, 2000, the night of the Bon Voyage Kahiki Party. The beautiful structure is gone, but is still living in the hearts and minds of many who visited her shores.
Listen now to the sound of a night out inside one of the greatest Polynesian restaurants in the world.
This album is dedicated to Marsh and Nina Padilla.
Special thanks to Lee Joseph and Carole Pixler, Tim Tsao and The Kahiki
Jeff Chenault 2010
Music Historian, Writer, Exotica DJ
Produced by Jeff Chenault
Mastered by Len Horowitz and Lee Joseph – History of Recorded Sound, Culver City, CA.
Graphic design: Carole Pixler carolepixler.com
Bacchus Archives – a part of the Dionysus Records Empire
www.dionysusrecords.com – an island of sounds awaits you!
Photo: Charles R. Moor, from the collection of Jeff Chenault, special thanks to Marcel Padilla
BACCHUS
Bacchus Archives BA11109

The back cover of the Beachcomber Trio's *Live at the Kahiki* album released on Dionysus Records. *Courtesy of Lee Joseph.*

Don Browne was a friend and member of the Beachcomber Trio and remembers Marsh fondly:

> *I played marimba and timbales in the Beachcomber Trio band in 1968. I played while I was a senior in the music school at Ohio State University and while I was a music teacher at New Albany High School.*
>
> *The Kahiki was a great place to visit and to work, and I met lots of great people there, including the staff from around the world and visitors from all over as well. Having the opportunity to play with some of the best musicians in Columbus, band leader, pianist, bassist and flutist Marsh Padilla and guitarist Leroy Plymale, was an experience I'll never forget.*

BOB "PULEVAI" WATERS

Hawaiian Entertainer

Bob Waters was born on November 9, 1922, in Covington, Kentucky, but he spent over twenty years entertaining guests at Howard Johnson's Hawaiian Village in Cincinnati. The son of a railroad engineer, Bob took an early liking to Hawaiian music, which would soon become his obsession and livelihood. While on vacation in 1939, Bob met Sam Koki, who was playing at Ken's Hula Hut in Los Angeles.

According to famous steel guitarist Jerry Byrd:

> *Bob and Sam became friends immediately. He took this country boy under his wing and taught him Hawaiian music and, at times, put him up in a cottage that was behind his own home. The aloha that Bob and Sam had for each other never faltered, and even though Bob's visits to California became less and less frequent, the warm friendship lasted until Sam passed away.*

It was Sam Koki who would later give Bob permission to use the name Paradise Islanders for his Hawaiian group in Cincinnati. Bob retired from the Paradise Islanders in 1986 and lived a good life until he passed away in 2006.

JERRY BYRD

Steel Guitar Player

Born in Lima, Ohio, on March 9, 1920, Gerald Lester Byrd, also known as Jerry Byrd, became known as the Master of the Steel Guitar. In Hawaiian circles, he was known simply as the Great One. In the early 1930s, Jerry fell in love with the sound of the Hawaiian steel guitar. Jerry even paid for instrument transcribing at the Honolulu Academy of Music in Lima, Ohio. He was playing professionally by the time he was fifteen. When Jerry graduated from high school, he left Lima to start his musical career. In the 1940s and 1950s, he accompanied some of the biggest names in country music, people like Hank Williams, Ernest Tubb and Patsy Cline, among others. In 1944, he joined the company of the Grand Ole Opry in Nashville. Jerry moved to Cincinnati in 1948 to play on radio and television

Right: It was a Trip on Wings of Music, a book written by Jerry Byrd. *Courtesy of Centerstream Publishing.*

Below: Byrd of Paradise album by Jerry Byrd, which was released on Monument Records in 1961. The cover girl's name is Miss Nalani Weeks. *Author's collection.*

shows for WLW. His first national television appearance was with the Pleasant Valley Boys on the *Midwestern Hayride* show. He also appeared on the *Straw Hat Matinee* twice a week; both shows were on NBC-TV. In 1952, he returned to Nashville and remained there for twenty years doing session recording and other radio and television appearances. While most of Jerry's early work was in country music, his true love was for Hawaiian music. In the early 1970s, he moved to Hawaii and worked on reviving the Hawaiian steel guitar music scene.

During an interview with Laurie Mills from the Canadian Broadcasting Company in 1973, Jerry talked about his Hawaiian influences:

> *I listened to the Hawaiians, because they were really the only ones who were playing the steel guitar at that time. Dick McIntyre was my particular favorite, although there were many great ones.…Andy Iona, Sam Koki, Sol Ho'oppi…all of them contributed to the steel guitar.* [There were] *a lot of kids like me* [who wanted to learn] *to play—but they couldn't play Hawaiian music in the middle of Ohio, so they played the next thing to come along, which was country music.*

In 1978, Jerry Byrd was the first steel guitar player to be inducted into the Steel Guitar Hall of Fame. In 2003, Jerry wrote his official biography *It Was a Trip on Wings of Music*. It chronicles his amazing lifelong career in music. Jerry passed away on April 11, 2005. His Rickenbacker lap steel guitar is still on display at the Country Music Hall of Fame. Today, the music of Jerry's steel guitar continues to evoke the true spirit of aloha.

FRANCIS LLACUNA

Hawaiian-Born Guitarist and Entertainer

For Francis Llacuna, his Hawaiian heritage runs deep. He was born on the island of Oahu, and his grandfather worked on the grounds of the original Hawaiian Village, when it was still the Niumali Hotel. Music came naturally for Francis, but musical opportunities in Hawaii were few and far between, so he moved to California. In the 1960s, Llacuna started working for the Tradewinds restaurant in Oxnard, California. His group was known as the International Four, and it consisted of Francis on guitar, Andre Cartier on

The talented singer, songwriter, storyteller and friend Francis Llacuna. *Author's collection.*

drums and two hula dancers, Eandi Haile and Bobbie Gentry. Yes, that Bobbie Gentry! The group would play in Las Vegas, Palm Springs and the Tahoe circuit.

Francis eventually moved to Ohio to be closer to family. While in Columbus, Francis played for various restaurants like the Tropical Bistro and Tai's Tiki. He played private parties like Dan Rockwell's famous Luau and the Call of the Tropics art show. Francis was also a regular entertainer for two large-scale Tiki events hosted by the Fraternal Order of Moai: the Hot Rod Hula Hop in Columbus, and Ohana Luau by the lake, in Lake George, New York.

9

TIKI ARTISTS

Ohio has produced an abundance of Tiki artists over the years. Self-taught Tiki carvers like Jim Robinson, black velvet painters like Robb Hamel and exotic lamp makers like John Holt all have found success in curating their Tiki art forms. Ohio has had two art shows that have showcased these artists and others. They reflect the ongoing Tiki culture in the state and continue to influence others. These are some of the artists that have used their unique abilities to bring a refreshing new look to Tiki culture.

JIM ROBINSON

Chisel Slinger

Jim Robinson is a veteran Tiki enthusiast, carver and musician. He is also one of the founding members of the Fraternal Order of Moai, which was started in Columbus in 2005. He is an active collector of all things Tiki, especially if it comes from the Kahiki. Jim and his wife, Elise, have collected some amazing artifacts from the Kahiki and are helping to preserve them for future generations. Elise even took care of the Kahiki parrot. Their backyard is a Tiki paradise; named the Rancho Kahiki Tiki Bar, it is a hidden oasis in the middle of suburbia. It's filled with nautical flotsam and jetsam, homemade carvings and an outside Tiki bar that Jim built himself.

Add a pool and some tropical plants and you have a complete backyard paradise. His basement bar has a complete South Seas nautical theme. It's loaded with faux waterfalls, fish tanks with tropical fish and portholes that give visitors the feeling of being in the hull of some ancient galleon ghost ship. Some of Robinson's private collection was featured in the book *Hula Dancers and Tiki Gods*, written by Chris Pfouts and published by Schiffer Publishing in 2001. Many of Robinson's Orchids of Hawaii lights came from the Kahiki, and they really give the space its charming ambiance. Bamboo furniture and homemade carvings fill the space as well. Jim started carving in the early 2000s and still carves today, albeit not as much as he used to. In his spare time, he plays lead guitar in his rockabilly band, Vegas 66, with Rex Xander on drums and Jeremy Clevenger on standup bass. Their music has a raunchy rockabilly style, like the Stray Cats but with an ass-kicking style all their own. Their CD *Wild Ride to Hell* is self-explanatory and highly recommended.

JOHN HOLT

Tikiskip

The Headhunters Club's dinner menus featured all kinds of exotic game from all over the world. *Courtesy of John Holt.*

John Holt Jr. is a former restaurateur and Tiki enthusiast. John used to own Jack's Diner in downtown Columbus, and his father owned it before him, so the restaurant business is in his blood. John's father, John T. Holt was an early restaurateur in Columbus, Ohio; he owned four restaurants: two were called Jack's, one was called Small Fry on State Street and another was called Golden Point on Oakland Park. John bought the Curly Cue diner in Pearl Alley in 1976, and he renamed it Jack's Diner. He ran the restaurant for twenty-two years before passing away in 1988. John's wife, Ida, ran the restaurant until 1993, when their son, John Jr., took over the business. John ran Jack's Diner from 1993 to 2004, when he sold it. What's interesting is that John Holt Sr.

was also a big-game hunter and was one of the founding members of the Headhunters Club in Columbus. Even Jimmy Crum, the famous Columbus sports announcer, was one of the club's vice presidents.

Here is a little background information culled from the Headhunters Fourteenth Annual Game Dinner menu.

Headhunters' History

It was 1962, and some of the Columbus-area sportsmen, who had hunted and fished in Africa, Asia, India, Mexico, South America and many other distant places, were drawn together by their common interest. Due largely to the efforts of Orr Zimmerman, the group, which came to be known as the Headhunters Club, was brought together. For, as all hunters know, the thrill of telling someone about a hunt is second only to the hunt itself. These hunting stories would be told with as much fact or fiction as the audience will permit. The club, which is strictly social, holds regular meetings, but the one outstanding event each year is the Annual Game Banquet. The club sponsors no group or person, and no one contributes to the event or sponsors the organization. The club's membership is limited and only

The Headhunters Club's official flag from Columbus, Ohio. *Courtesy of John Holt.*

The Tiki Skip logo was created by the ever-talented Sam Gambino. *Courtesy of John Holt.*

to those who have hunted outside the continental United States can receive an invitation to join.

The first three Game Banquets were held at the Athletic Club of Columbus, and they were spectacular affairs. The menus offer dishes that are adventures themselves. Dishes served at the banquet are concocted from game brought back from members' hunting trips and safaris. The last ten dinners have been held at the Darby Dan Farm.

At the first banquets, members of this exclusive club brought back big game and fish to be prepared by the Darby Dan Farm chefs for a huge dinner around Christmastime. The lobby of Darby Dan's had many stuffed trophy animals from around the globe. According to John, they even had a "real" shrunken head!

John also was a huge fan of the Kahiki. Going there for drinks with his favorite bartender Skip (hence his nickname) was one of his favorite pastimes. John not only loves Tiki culture, but he's a Tiki artist as well. He started making Polynesian-style lights for his own bar in 2005. Then, others started asking him to make lights for them. His most popular lights are the Skip Float; a Skip Float is made from a light of his own design and regular fish floats tied together with rope. John has made lights for Sven Kirsten, Tiki Ti, Tropical Bistro, Frankie's Las Vegas, the Tonga Hut and, more recently, the Tiki Underground. As of 2018, John has made over 165 lights; he still makes lights today but mostly as a fun hobby for himself.

DON DRENNAN

Artist Don Drennan has worked in a wide variety of arts and disciplines—from sculpting foam and designing in Photoshop to doing computer animations. He built a six-foot replica of the Kahiki fireplace for the Tropical Bistro, which he also does commissions for. I personally have

A handmade Tiki mask made by Don Drennan. *Courtesy of Carmen Owens.*

one of his fireplaces in my basement. Don also contributed a lot to the decoration of the Grass Skirt Tiki Bar, including masks and other South Seas objects. One of the things Don enjoys is creating models for 3D printing. He uses the original plastic mugs to make molds for his own ceramic Tiki mugs. Don has created many mugs over the years, including the famous Beaver Tiki.

ROBB HAMEL

During the mid-2000s, Robb was one of the most highly acclaimed black velvet artists in the United States. For a few short years, his art gained high praise in the Tiki community for his spectacular attention to detail. During the making of this book, I could not locate Robb Hamel, but his work will always be remembered as some of the best in the genre.

10

TIKI AND RUM ORGANIZATIONS

THE FRATERNAL ORDER OF MOAI

The Fraternal Order of Moai (FOM) was founded by Matt Thatcher (Kuku Ahu) and Jim Robinson (Chisel Slinger) in 2005. The group is an Ohio nonprofit corporation whose national charity is the Easter Island Foundation. Its core values are good works, fellowship, spirit, presence, preservation and celebration. Today, it boasts ten nationwide chapters. Its goal is to serve as the premier fraternal organization and social network for men and women interested in Tiki culture and the historical aspects of Polynesian Pop. They are also interested in preservation and donate to various local charities. Every August, the Kahiki chapter in Columbus holds a Tiki-themed event called the Hula Hop. It is a full day of festivities that includes Polynesian food, tropical cocktails, craft beer, food trucks and Tiki vendors from all over the country. They also have creative entertainment and live music booths both inside the Grass Skirt and on its outdoor stage. Admission to these events is free, and all proceeds are donated to Cure CMD, a nonprofit organization that was formed by parents whose children have been affected by congenital muscular dystrophy. The Hula Hop is a party with a purpose. More information about the Hula Hop can be found at the website www.hulahopcolumbus.com.

A ticket for the Feast of the Tiki Gods dinner party, which was part of the Hot Rod Hula Hop event in Columbus, Ohio. *Author's collection.*

INTERVIEW WITH MATT THATCHER

Kuku Ahu

This interview was conducted on January 14, 2019, by Jeff Chenault.

JEFF CHENAULT. Did you ever visit the Kahiki?

MATT THATCHER. Absolutely. Many times. I remember family trips to the Kahiki…when I was five years old in 1977. Sitting in the thatched roof booths with a Shirley Temple in hand [that was] *served in a red plastic cup was very likely what began my obsession with Tiki culture. I would beg my parents and grandparents to let me have a Coco Joe's Tiki from the gift shop every time we went there. I still have several of those.*

JEFF. How did you get interested in Polynesian Pop?

MATT. I never really thought of Tiki or Polynesian Pop as being a certain cultural thing any more than one considers the origin of a cheeseburger. The Kahiki and the Tiki Room at Walt Disney World were just things I grew up with and maybe even took for granted. Speaking in terms of discovering that there was a culture of Tiki aficionados, that didn't happen until after they shuttered the Kahiki. Suddenly, this part of my childhood was swept away, and it upset me considerably. As a consequence, I went searching for other people who felt the same way.

147

JEFF. What made you and Jim Robinson decide to form the FOM?

MATT. Jim and I were both looking for other Tikiphiles in our locale when we met, and we just started riffing off of each other over drinks. Let's not forget Joel Gunn in that formative stage; he was quintessential in making things a reality and came on board right after Jim and I first had a few brainstorm sessions. I think we were also, at the time, three creative types suffering a bit of artistic burn out that just happened to coincide with the Kahiki closure. Our rather lofty, and honestly, a bit nutty ideas just seemed like one hell of a terrific creative endeavor that might make the world a tiny bit better if we could pull it off. It was a social experiment as well as a somewhat tongue-in-cheek bit of performance art. When it exploded very early in terms of interest, we were always just barely keeping up. Those early days were a whirlwind of hard work and fantastic times.

JEFF. Are you surprised by how much the FOM has grown over the years?

MATT. Every single day. It's simply amazing to me that our strange plan would evolve into something so wonderful and vast. I could never take credit for what the Moai have become and what they have accomplished. It has truly taken a village, and we have some of the best and brightest in our midst. We had some crazy ideas that got it rolling, but the Fellowship has earned all the credit for making it a reality.

JEFF. Has the FOM become what you envisioned thirteen years ago?

MATT. Fourteen years, now, to be exact. To be honest, it has become far more than I would have expected at any one point in its formation, that's for sure. The concept was ever evolving in those earliest days; we worked hard just to stay slightly ahead. The directions members have taken us at this point far exceed what I ever imagined might happen in my lifetime. Some of the best times I have had in my life have been because of, and with, my Fellow Moai.

JEFF. What is a Honui?

MATT. In the simplest terms, a Honui is a fellow Moai who has earned their fez. Honui means "honored one," and we all take that honor very seriously. The fez is our most visible public symbol, and it identifies a fellow immediately when worn. As such, it is important to us that those who are so visible represent the most accomplished and committed of us.

JEFF. Recently, the Hot Rod Hula Hop changed its identity to just The Hula Hop. Why the name change? What's the focus of the event now?

MATT. The Hula Hop, as it is presented today, is actually closer to what I was looking to do back in 2005 when we held the first event. The Hula Hop is much more Tiki-centric and local now that it shares less stage with the custom culture elements of the past. Don't get me wrong, I love the hot rods and classic cars as much as ever, but we have the luxury of having a more focused event in one location: The Grass Skirt Tiki Room. We were also faced with changing demographics that seemed to be affecting interest in certain aspects of the event, and when you raise money for charity, the cost versus donation equation is always on the forefront in your mind. We decided to evolve, and it just happened that we could evolve toward what I wanted originally anyway. So, it's a win-win really, and the Hula Hop has been a huge success since the change. Feedback is extremely positive, and we are able to contribute a sizable donation to CureCMD more reliably now.

JEFF. What would you like to see the FOM do in the future?

MATT. Ha! Hmm…colonize another planet and create the largest Tiki bar humanity has ever known! In all seriousness, I just want to see the Moai continue to grow, raise more money for good causes, and have a lot of fun in the process. We have proven that this model works, and I would like to see it continue and prosper indefinitely.

OHIO RUM SOCIETY

The Central Ohio Rum Society, which is now known simply as the Ohio Rum Society, logo. *Courtesy of Chad White.*

This group, founded by Chad White, is the premier group for all things rum in Ohio. Since most Polynesian cocktails use rum as the primary ingredient, his presence in the state is most welcome. Chad has done a tremendous amount of work educating people on rum culture. From the harvesting of sugar cane to the proper mix and balance of various rums, his knowledge is extensive as his rum collection.

The Ohio Rum Society (ORS) was established in August 2016. It was originally an outlet for founder Chad White to share his passion for cane spirits in a city still hooked on vodka and bourbon. White quickly learned of the incredible symbiotic relationship between rum and Tiki, and that is what ultimately attracted him, because it tied in with his love of travel, history and the craft cocktail movement at the time. Rum is the most diverse and historically rich spirit in the world, yet it is also the most underappreciated and misunderstood. Chad was committed to changing the public's perception of rum while also carving out his own corner in the local cocktail scene. After a few months of private tastings at his home and stoking forum discussions on the group's Facebook page, the first ORS meet-and-greet was held on November 2016 at the Grass Skirt Tiki Room. White hosted the event with the help of Brian Maxwell and Liza Farrell, both former Grass Skirt bartenders.

According to Chad, the mission of Ohio Rum Society is twofold:

1. To elevate the rum category in the (liquor control) state of Ohio and empower consumers via interactive education and knowledge sharing,

2. To showcase the best cocktail programs and bartending talent in Columbus.

But like rum itself, it's a bit more complicated than that. As an access point, ORS exists to educate bartenders on the most diverse spirit in the world. To empower the consumers of Ohio to make better decisions at their local liquor "control agency." To debunk the myths and destroy the stigma attached to rum and its relatives. To enlighten the general public of the vast world of cane spirits and the plethora of styles waiting to be explored on the palate, neat or tinkered with in cocktails. There's a lot of confusion to be cleared and tons of rocks to be turned over, and this is the purpose of the Ohio Rum Society.

The rum revolution has been gaining steam over the last ten to fifteen years due to help from the craft cocktail movement and the resurgence of Tiki in America. For more information on the Ohio Rum Society, please visit their Facebook page.

BIBLIOGRAPHY

Batz, Bob. "Fruitful, Produce Patriarchs of Dayton Recall Freshness of a Simpler Era." *Dayton Daily News*, March 20, 1983.

Byrne, James. "Ex-Actor Happy in Business." *Cincinnati Enquirer*, August 27, 1967.

Chillicothe Gazette. "Tahiti Restaurant Advertisement." September 15, 1967.

Cincinnati Enquirer. "Dancers Open Club." December 2, 1954.

———. "Hawaiian Luau Anniversary Today." October 27, 1979.

———. "H.J. Opens Pavilion." October 11, 1965.

———. "The Lure of the Luau." July 24, 1965.

———. "Miami Designer Believes in 'Design in Depth.'" April 10, 1964.

———. "Polynesian Adventure." July 3, 1965.

———. "Who Needs Hula If Food Is Exotic in $220,000 Room?" August 20, 1965.

Cincinnati Post. "Judge Rules Go-Go Dancers Employees." January 18, 1974.

Cincinnati Post & Times-Star. "Fashions with Food at Exotic Kon-Tiki." February 18, 1972.

———. "Hawaiian Luau Is New Feature at Netherland." October 15, 1971.

Cinema Treasures. www.cinematreasures.org.

Clark, Bill. "Goodie Sable to Mark 70th Among the Stars." *Dayton Daily News*, December 24, 1967.

Columbus Dispatch. "Tai Tiki—Tasteful Newcomer Dishes up Polynesian Cuisine, Memories." July 16, 2015.

Daily Reporter. "Beachcomber Supper Club in Canton Advertisement." June 5, 1964.

Dayton Daily News. "Restaurant Décor Change Under Study." October 26, 1960.
———. "Sable, RKO Chief Here, Leaving Theatre Chain." October 14, 1953.
———. "Tropics Restaurant is Wrecked by Fire." April 15, 1953.
DeCamp, Graydon. "Dancing Go-Go Girls Picket Tahiki Lounge." *Cincinnati Post & Times-Star*, July 3, 1969.
Detroit Free Press. "The Tropics Opening, June 15, 1941." June 16, 1941.
Downing, Bob. "Waikiki a Little Too Close to China." *Akron Beacon Journal*, February 5, 1981.
Evening Independent (Massillon, OH). "Beachcomber Will Reopen." January 30, 1971.
———. "Polynesian Restaurant Holds Grand Opening." January 17, 1976.
Filipic, Martha. "Small City Lures Owner of Restaurant from Capital." *Chillicothe Gazette*, August 10, 1985.
Fox, Ryan Justin. "High Hopes for Kon-Tiki Site." *Dayton Daily News*, January 5, 2005.
Fulwider, William. "Designers Produce Warm, Graceful Spot." *Columbus Evening Dispatch*, September 7, 1963.
Gordon, Richard L. "Lights Dim on Jobs, Pleasure, History…" *Cincinnati Post*, June 13, 1974.
Hall, Stephen S. J. "The Specialty Restaurant—Sheraton-Cleveland's Kon-Tiki." *Cornell Hospitality Quarterly*, May 1, 1961.
Historic Hotels of America. "Hilton Cincinnati Netherland Plaza." www.historichotels.org.
Hively, Sue. "Safari Island Animals Exist on Exotic Foods." *Sandusky Register*, August 16, 1965.
Jones, Jack. "Little Polynesia at Dobbs' Airport Lounge." *Dayton Daily News*, June 21, 1959.
Kany, A.S. "Let's Go Places." *Journal Herald* (Dayton, OH), November 1, 1954.
Knout, Jo Ann. "As Always Goodie Will Be There." *Dayton Daily News*, December 31, 1974.
Lancaster Eagle Gazzette. "Fred Eaton's Castaway Advertisement." April 14, 1979.
———. "Tiki Restaurant Offers Atmosphere, Peace." November 15, 1975.
Myers, Jim. "Former Merchant Seaman Turns Passion to Profit." *Dayton Daily News*, June 16, 1960.
Newark Advocate. "Fire Hits Lounge on West Side." April 20, 1967.
———. "New Polynesian Lounge Will Open in 3 Weeks." June 7, 1966.

News-Journal (Mansfield, OH). "Applications Being Taken for Kahona Club." February 13, 1966.

———. "Cedar Point to Open 96th Season." May 21, 1965.

———. "Jungle Larry Booked at Cedar Point." January 13, 1965.

Osler, Jack M. "Hawaiian Vacations." *Dayton Leisure*, October 19, 1980.

Pierce, Phyl. "And Incidentally." *Dayton Daily News*, May 2, 1948.

Price, Lyle W. "Barney West Famous for Tricky Tikis." *Gettysburg Times*, December 23, 1965.

Radcliffe, E.B. "Inscrutable Chinese?!" *Cincinnati Enquirer*, February 21, 1961.

Radel, Cliff. "Aloha! From the Sunny Isle of Sharonville." *Cincinnati Enquirer*, April 17, 1980.

Raiser, Moe. "He Carves South Sea Gods from Redwood Logs." *Paducah Sun*, January 20, 1961.

Ruymar, Lorene, and Joe Boyd. "Hawaiian Steel Guitar and Its Hawaiian Musicians." *Centerstream Publications*, August 1, 1996.

Sandusky Register. "A Bosom Buddy to Animals." June 12, 1965.

———. "Cedar Point Gets 'New' Look For '65." April 3, 1965.

Snow, Jane. "Beachcomber's Emphasis: Seafood." *Akron Beacon Journal*, February 2, 1984.

Stevens, Dale. "Cantonese Chicken Velvet Draws Diners to Kali-Kai." *Cincinnati Post & Times-Star*, June 16, 1967.

———. "Club Owner Tackles the Recording Field." *Cincinnati Post & Times-Star*, April 20, 1966.

———. "Dining Out—Kali-Kai." *Cincinnati Post & Times-Star*, September 30, 1966.

———. "Hawaiian Village Has, of all Things, Hawaiians." *Cincinnati Post & Times-Star*, January 29, 1965.

———. "Howard Johnson's Hawaiian Village Bursts Its Pool-Side Walls." *Cincinnati Post & Times-Star*, October 15, 1965.

———. "Kon-Tiki's Buffet Rousing Success." *Cincinnati Post & Times-Star*, January 23, 1970.

———. "Rudin Expands Tropics in Entertainment Hypo." *Dayton Daily News*, December 23, 1951.

———. "Savory Changing to Polynesian Luau." *Cincinnati Post & Times-Star*, March 26, 1965.

———. "Sheraton-Gibson Introduces South Seas Food Monday." *Cincinnati Post & Times-Star*, August 20, 1965.

Tamor, Phyllis. "Crane Plays Host the Polynesian Way." *Cincinnati Enquirer*, August 26, 1965.

BIBLIOGRAPHY

Thrasher, Don. "Tiki Time—Call of the Tropics Celebrates Mid-20th Century Culture." *Dayton Daily News*, July 6, 2012.

Toledo Blade. "Ex-Owner's Aku-Aku Club Drew Crowds, Raves." February 2, 2002.

Williams, Mardo. "Deshler Hilton Plans Third Plush Restaurant." *Columbus Evening Dispatch*, September 6, 1963.

INDEX

ABOUT THE AUTHOR

J eff Chenault is an author, producer and music historian. His first book, *Kahiki Supper Club: A Polynesian Paradise in Columbus, Ohio*, was published by The History Press and co-written with David Meyers, Elise Meyers-Walker and Doug Motz. Jeff has also written for multiple publications including *Cool and Strange Music Magazine*, *Bachelor Pad Magazine*, *Tiki Magazine* and *Exotica Moderne*. He is currently producing a series of rare exotica albums for Dionysus Records.